RIGHT STORY,
WRONG STORY

How to Have Fearless
Conversations in Hell

Tyson Yunkaporta

HarperOne

An Imprint of HarperCollins*Publishers*

HarperCollins books may be purchased for educational, business, or sales promotional use. For information, please email the Special Markets Department at SPsales@harpercollins.com.

Originally published in Australia in 2023 by Text Publishing.

First HarperOne paperback published in 2026

harpercollins.com

Design adapted from the Text Publishing edition

Library of Congress Cataloging-in-Publication Data is available upon request.

ISBN 978-0-06-338234-3

25 26 27 28 29 LBC 5 4 3 2 1

For my sweet, sweet woman.
Sorry about the mess and thank you for all the love magic.

Contents

The Wrong Canoe

Hello my sibling.

Did you know that male echidnas have four penises? If I were as smart as an echidna, I could use that factoid to come up with an evolutionary theory about male dominance and project it onto my own species, then sell a truckload of books. It's not really a fact though—he only has one grotesque dick with four heads, and his mate probably doesn't want that horrible thing anywhere near either of her vaginas.

I couldn't deliberately misinform you like that for profit. You and I have the same mother (you're standing on her right now), so it would be unthinkable for me to deploy some pseudo-scientific influencer trickery to twist your mind and ruin your life, just so I can make some money. Us-two are related!

We have plenty in common that we can build on to strengthen our relationship here, as we journey through a suite of pathologies that need some attention before we destroy the world with our dysfunction. Even if you don't have the same disorders as me, you probably belong to a culture that does, unless of course you're from a healthy culture (in which case your land has almost certainly been invaded by an unhealthy one that will break you soon anyway). Either way, we both need to work on our issues, because no tree burns alone.

My brother says it's our fault as Indigenous people that the world is dying, because we've failed to bring settlers into proper relation. Many of us would hate him for saying this (which is why he doesn't want to be named here). I don't much like hearing it myself, because I have historical IOUs I want to cash in pronto now the barman's calling last drinks. But I still listen to him because we're related.

This book contains nothing that will save the world. It's basically a list of twelve ways to avoid lists in the Anthropocene, some jokes and horror stories. Also a few attempts at good sense that future alien archaeologists can dig up to discover that most homo sapiens were not stupid, greedy bastards—we just had very bad bosses.

It is always comforting to know that your smug ghost

will be able to drift around a blasted landscape forever, wheezing, 'I tooooold you sooooo!' However this kind of death wish is not the best mindset for trying to make meaning together. We're going to need to do more than merely ask each other *RUOK?* just because there's a poster in the staff toilet telling us we should. We need to heal a little, and we need to do it together because it's going to hurt like hell.

Us-two will have yarns with many people as we journey through fire and water and rock. In my community, yarning is like conversation, but with the futile and passive-aggressive parts removed. The closest equivalent in western culture I can find is thought experiment, which is a ritualised crowdsourced narrative where everyone contributes their insight to the story and every contribution is honoured and included, no matter how contradictory these points of view might seem.

This chapter and the last one will be like the green room at a big event: a place to hang out with galaxy-brain thinkers like Hobbes and Rousseau and try to decide what we want to believe about the human condition. Discordant ideas will sting us like hornets and horrific realities will drain our hope like leeches. Then we'll take a walk through a blackwood forest full of vengeful trees, followed by a descent through nine circles of hell on Earth. Us-two can compare notes in the green room here at the start and again at the end if we make it through, to see if we've healed or grown at all on the journey. I have no map or story for this foolish narrative of the hero's journey (just a few notes from my friend Dante), and I don't know what kind of person you are, so we're steering into a storm here like a couple of drunks who met at a tavern and stole a boat together.

Maybe you're one of those people who is into inspirational self-help, New Age woo-woo and native wisdom. Gosh, you're going to be disappointed. Personal development (like development in general) is a combination of the stupidest parts of science and the stupidest parts of spirituality, and I think it has hastened the death of the planet over the last century. But that opinion is just part of my story—yours is equally important, so I'm happy to find you here. I'm not going to be doing any trust falls, vison quests, meditation or breathing exercises with you, though. Sorry.

Come sit down and have a *kapati* (cup of tea), because we're going to science the shit out of this messed-up world right now, and that job, like all jobs, is best begun with a yarn around the hearth. Data says nothing without analysis, and analysis is always guided by narratives. Always. So bring your stories round the fire here because we need all our stories to make this analysis work, including yours.

You are welcome. Even if you're a toxic, bad-faith, murderous, gaslighting piece of shit, you are needed and you are loved. We're on flat country here, with no moral high ground to be won. And you won't have to worry about feeling inadequate in the company of some paragon of ancient wisdom. That's not me having low self-esteem—I belong to a culture where everyone is taken care of, and nobody is above anybody else. I'm quite comfortable with my shortcomings and my limited cultural role. I know that no matter what, I will be loved and respected and cared for, and this certainty allows me to meet all of my obligations— even, on occasion, exceed my limits and write something interesting.

I'd like to offer you the same kind of relation, even though I probably won't be able to deliver on it in person. I would if I could. I'd be your brother and love you, and there are plenty of people who would do the same, so look around for them before you do anything that can't be undone. You are cared for, potentially, so come find us caring people. Hot tip—the best way to do that is to start being a caring person.

All my friends are here, and I respect every one of them, whether they are living or not. My buddies Hobbes and Rousseau are both here. You know them too? Hobbes said our ancestors had short lives of brutish misery and primitive ignorance, and Rousseau said they were noble savages living in paradise. But they're together here, sitting at the edge of the firelight, scared, confused; crying as they awkwardly start kissing. They'll be fine. We'll all be fine, okay?

I'm told people are interested in my writing purely for the things I can get away with saying only because of my exotic identity. I have friends who tell me that free speech is available to me and not them, because I belong to the

Apalech Clan from the remote far north of Australia and they don't. And because their ancestors were removed from their homelands sometime in the last few centuries and mine were dispossessed more recently. And I have a 'special' connection to the land, and they don't.

Well, I've never said all that, but I can't stop them from projecting it on me. I do love our Aboriginal culture and I think it is the best way to live that has ever existed on this earth, but I'm not here to defend or promote that point of view.

All I know is that we're all scared and tired, and we desperately need to take a break (as well as some urgent action). So take an active, urgent break and enjoy this experience built from the fresh corpses of trees, or powered by the not-so-fresh corpses of trees long dead (depending on whether you have a paper or digital copy). If I sell enough, I'm going to get a small block of Aboriginal land back, just enough for the kids and a few chickens to run around on while we wait for the drones and bulldozers and superstorms to come.

This experience is a masterclass in some sort of indigenised hipster pop science I've fallen arse-backwards into over the last few years not because it's righteous or rigorous, but because people like it and it's fun. It makes sarcasm into a dialectical art form we practise together as reader and writer, in which we perform scepticism to highlight our faith, play the disruptive trickster to foster stability, mourn the end to celebrate the beginning. And randomly mash opposite ideas together in order to cultivate the illusion of ancient wisdom…But seriously: together we'll find that it's not the content that matters—it's the process and the relation. For that, we have to bring our stories together. Take a minute to retrieve one of your stories, then, if you want to proceed, let it weave in with a story from the web of relationships that is me.

Here is my *kinuw* story. Just be aware that the translation of Aboriginal language pronouns into English might feel strange, but the story won't work in some places without us-two, us-only, us-all, and so forth. Don't have a heart attack—I'm not going to force you to use my Indigenous pronouns. In our culture you can't force anyone to do anything.

> You might find yourself in a story-place now, in a site of totemic relation with the waterlilies that grow near a river. The seeds from that lily have been ground to make bread for tens of thousands of years. You and that plant species are kin, and you-two are being moved into a season of abundance following a period of heavy rain. The land is moving you in its annual cycles, directing you towards diets and activities that you need to be healthy and complete. But there are longer cycles at play here, too.
>
> Nearby there is a particular tree that only flowers once or twice in a century, and it is in full bloom right now. You've never seen this before, but

the old people with you remember it. Under that tree, a crocodile is nesting so we-all avoid that part of the river today, and a dozen of your nephews and nieces are splashing in the shallows on a different riverbank, where the old people say it is safe this morning (but not tomorrow morning). You don't have to follow their instructions because there are no bosses here, but you listen to those old people if you don't want to get bitten. We-all live the old stories that guide us in listening respectfully, so we don't have to worry about predators. The strange new story of fight or flight that is associated with Palaeolithic life is absent here, because you-all know where the predators are, always. They are your relations.

The last time the old people saw that tree flowering at the crocodile's nest was also the last time a dugout canoe was made in this place. They want to make sure everyone remembers how to do this, so that is why you-all are here today. While the children play, some people are casting nets for bait fish while others are loading up a rusty barge with water, tools and handlines for fishing. Soon everyone is crowded on board and you-all are on your way inland to the canoe tree the old people have carefully selected for this day.

On the way you-all stop to pick up some aunties who have been collecting shellfish and crabs in the mangroves. They call out where to stop there, and the authority in the group shifts to a grandmother who advises you-all during this leg of the journey, because this part of the river is her place. She sits with you awhile and you-two watch a dolphin at play while she tells you its story. It is called *otamat*, which she tells you is an old word that came from an international trading relationship with Indonesia a long time ago. She also tells you that this historical trading relation with New Guinea and Indonesia influenced the design of the canoe you-all are going to make today.

Around a few river bends, and the authority shifts again to the man who speaks for the place where the canoe tree lives. But the group doesn't follow his instructions right away, as there are white birds diving into the river near the far bank, so you-all know there are fat white fish feeding in that spot too. Everyone decides to go fish there for a while to get more food for later. Some split off and move to the riverbank to make a fire and cook some of those white fish. Eventually they return and the river moves you-all further inland.

On the last leg of the journey, you sit with your nephew and teach him the names of dozens of orchids growing in the mangroves. It's the first time he has noticed these plants, but now that he knows their names he will see them every time. One of those orchids contains a substance that can turn salt water into fresh water, and you could probably patent that plant's genetic sequence and make a billion dollars, if you were some kind of devil. There are people who would pay you a fortune just to keep it a secret. Or kill you for it. Best to keep that to ourselves, maybe.

Soon the barge lands at the site of the canoe tree and everyone splits off to do whatever they like. Your young cousin chases a puppy with a stick and then goes all sooky when you growl at him. You-all fish for bream and you leave your line in too long, so an aquatic file snake grabs the bream you've hooked and you get a two-for-one deal on your lunch. Aunties begin collecting shiny red seeds for decorating cultural objects, seeds that have been used for thousands of years for birth control. This doesn't sit well with what your teachers at school told you about modern medicine recently liberating women for the first time in human history with the invention of the birth control pill. You might think about how much that would change things if everyone understood the implications, except it's just a lovely day and you're experiencing pure joy at being away from all the institutions and officers who run your life, if only for a day. So you stop thinking so much and just feel, and be in relation with family and place.

You-all take turns with the axe to fell the canoe tree. A few swings then pass it on. It is trimmed and cut to size then tied to the barge while you eat the file snake and hear the story of her part in the tale of Taipan and Blue-Tongue Lizard. The places in that story find their way into your mental map of that country, as you-all pack up and head for home, dragging the canoe tree behind.

Back at the waterlily place, you eat crabs for dinner and feel a tap on your shoulder and turn to see that nobody is there. The shoulder is the corresponding body part for your father-child relation, so you worry about your dad. Someone drives up from town and you get the news that he's all right, but not happy that you took his spear this morning without letting him know. You look around for that spear but somebody else took it at lunchtime and after that you lost track of where it went. A sharing economy is no guarantee of harmony, and there is going to be trouble with your dad later. Big trouble. But that's later, so forget about it for now and enjoy the sunset and the crabs.

Next morning, the old men start shaping the canoe with axes, digging it out and burning it out with fire. You watch for a long time until you definitely know how to do it, then join in. There's no trial and error here, no 'learning from mistakes'. A person either knows how to do something or doesn't, and learns it by listening and looking. The self-other boundary between you-all and the adept carvers is so fluid that you-all are not just observing them-all, but being them-all, and so you learn and demonstrate mastery on the first attempt.

It is the same learning process when you go with a select kin-group (us-only) to cut the oars and outrigging in the mangroves. The mangrove is a naturally perfect shape for an oar, and it doesn't take many cuts to finish. Mangrove and oar have the same name, a strange-sounding word that doesn't feel like it fits with your language, and you wonder if this is also a word that came from overseas trade long ago.

Next day the canoe is finished, and this is the time for the children. There are dozens there now, paddling the canoe in the shallows and doing backflips off it, laughing and screaming. This is the best part.

The family uses the canoe over the next few months, but then it is collected and placed on display in an institution that owns it now. Insects start eating it from the inside out and its new owners spray it with chemicals to preserve it, but too late. The insect eggs were deep in the wood like a self-destructing message in a spy movie. Our vessel needs to be living and in regular use in fresh and salt water to stop the insects from eating it away. It soon crumbles to sawdust and someone writes a paper lamenting the demise of 'the last canoe'.

They don't get it. The canoe is not a belonging. The belonging is in the relationships that were strengthened in the canoe's making, and the knowledge processes of a thousand activities that were demonstrated and passed on to the next generation at the same time. As long as the relationships last, the maps and blueprints of the canoe will remain as living knowledge that will outlast all the books and all the servers that might try to capture this story. Relationships are the only way to store data safely in the long term.

In my culture you seldom hear a story packaged this way into a beginning, middle and end sequence with a clear theme and moral messages. If you're fishing in the place where an avian ancestor died, you hear that part of the story and any relevant information for fishing there in that season. Maybe you'll be given a message about jealousy too, if that's been a problem for you lately. You might not hear about the egg part of that story until years later, when it's pertinent for some other action or transgression in a specific time and place.

That *kinuw* story I just told might make sense to you, but not to me. The actual events took place in a different sequence, in different seasons and over a longer period of time. I read that story and I see some relationships of place and people out of step with each other and it's confusing as hell. But I wrote it for you, adjusting my whole world to demonstrate understanding and respect for cultural logic sequences that are different from my own.

I can't ask you to read on through an entire book of what will feel like disconnected narrative fragments and chaotic collages of segmented and contradictory conversations without showing that respect first. There are provocations we will be navigating together that are dangerous and unsettling, but we can't do that unless we're coming into relation first in a space of translation that is neither mine nor yours, but that us-two build together as we go along. Because that relationship together is all we've got, and someday soon everyone will have to realise that if we want to continue living.

There's not much going on inside of you or me as individuals. Not much at all. Like me, you've probably had family, mentors, coaches, authors, teachers and algorithmically tailored content telling you the opposite of that for years. Maybe they told you that inside you there is a unique being of hidden depths, fabulous talents, bespoke traumas and a demographic profile of privileges and disadvantages that determines your individual fate. Maybe they gave you a mask and called it a face.

So you imagine that entity into being, and right now it is riding your body around like a horse, a complex but flawed rider who is desperately lonely and in need of endless personal development and affirmation. Your rider needs to be heard. Your rider needs to do breath-work. Your rider needs to learn cultural humility. Your rider needs to self-actualise.

Maybe we're so much less complicated (and more complex) than that, us humans. Maybe we just have basic operating protocols hardwiring us to interact with our landscape, to graze on information from our country, language and culture until we grow a relational net that can collectively process complexity, a mind extending beyond the skull as far as our storied maps of being can go. Perhaps when we create, think, feel or communicate we are only able to do so to the limits of these relational nets.

Consider the possibility that you're nothing without your relations. All your kin—human, non-human, plant, animal, place, blood, water—all these familial links contain your thinking and character, the things you have always imagined to be occurring inside your fabulous individual mind. Ponder the notion that there is almost nothing you can learn about ants by examining a single specimen in a petri dish. It's a good frame for thinking, realising that even an entire ant colony can't yield much useful insight unless you know the system of seasons, waterways, species and symbiotic relations in which that colony sits. Well, I've found that frame useful anyway, when investigating colonies.

I wrote a book once called *Sand Talk*, and because there's no room for 150 co-authors on a book cover, everyone assumed that the words were my own. They weren't. Every thought in there came from a relationship and sits still in that relation, connecting out to new knowledge-families every day. Its pages hold nothing, just as I hold nothing. The chapters were all carved into traditional objects before they were written, and then part of the story in those tools and weapons was translated into print. But the true knowledge was (and still is) carried in the relationships.

So you need to know my relations first—not just the local view but how everything fits into the real world, the wider world.

I'm a younger sibling. My elder sister Delys speaks for me, and my big brother Steve speaks for the stories we carry together. There are a lot of brothers and sisters and cousins, and when we see each other in the distance some of us might call out, 'Brolga brolga brolga!' and answer, 'Kor' kor' kor'!' because that crane is a bird that binds us in common totemic relation. That doesn't mean everything is peaceful though. Families fight, families split, families harm, and these days the old mechanisms aren't always in place to stop this. Like everybody in the world, we are struggling right now. There is no sovereign paradise to be found anymore—just mining and pastoral leases encircling villages where the only growth industry is policing.

Dad is known as Rambo because he was wild like me in his youth. He is a church elder now. Mum passed away a few years back. But there are lots of mums and lots of dads, as their brothers and sisters are known to me in this way, and they all grew us up. They only started raising me (as an Aboriginal boy of orphan/tribeless status) in my late twenties, so I'm a bit of a late developer, even though I'm fifty now. My siblings and I grow up our own children and a lot of nephews, nieces and grandchildren, who also have children that we all care for together, often taking them with us in our travels. This is most of our work. The rest is acquiring enough money to feed, shelter, equip and educate everyone. Sometimes there is time to care for country and do ceremony, too. But not much.

We all try really hard, but I tell you, I'm sick of hearing this rubbish statistic about eighty per cent of the world's remaining biodiversity being diligently cared for by Indigenous Peoples. Most of us have only nominal Native Title and no real control, 'co-managing' the land at best, in ways that facilitate mining or agricultural interests, while we struggle to feed and shelter ourselves in the economy of the occupying culture. That doesn't leave us much time to look after the shred of biodiversity left in their water reserves, agriculture complexes, real-estate developments and mining leases. Our family does continue this work in our sacred places (the ones that haven't yet been blown up or bulldozed), but it is very hard to cram it all into a weekend.

Our brolga story is connected to a sacred site called Moving Stone, and also a lot of other places along that songline—the narrative map in the landscape that holds clan knowledge and history. This also connects us to the Rainbow Serpent, lightning, storm, blood, urine, waterlily, mudshell, black cockatoo and more. These are all entities that exist in relation with us.

We are linked to other families in other clans as well, along with many people from other areas far afield. We often travel and stay in these places with them, sometimes for many years. We often adopt or marry into those places and families and stay there forever. One of my many nieces is currently going through the process of full customary adoption into a family in another community. She will take on their name and bloodlines, and we will be sad to lose her, but also happy to be strengthening connections and interdependent relations with this other Country. In our culture we know this is the best way to avoid the emergence of imperialism and industrial warfare—which is why we've always had battles, but never had wars. Adoption and marriage across groups is a sacred thing, and it works better for us than it does in *Game of Thrones*. I have one uncle who went to Mornington Island years ago and never came back! But that was about a woman...

Same thing happened to me recently, which is how I finished up 3,500 kilometres south of home, suddenly in the city but madly in love with my spouse Megan. We have two babies together now and I'm stepfather for her daughter too. Megan is related to the Smiths and Mitchells from the Baradha people in central Queensland. I think I fell in love with her because she has as many scars as I do, and that means we can read each other's bodies like Russian novels. She is an active participant in many of the yarns in this book.

I have both strong affiliations and older, broken ties with Indigenous relatives far from my home, many different relationships from distant relatives to close cultural connections, in the south and west of Australia. In healthy Aboriginal social contexts, we would say all these names upon introduction over the course of many hours or even days and nights, and try to figure out how we connect down to one degree of separation, so we know what to call each other in relational terms, but this isn't really possible for the international audience reading these words, so I might leave that protocol out. I've already worn out my welcome in the word-length of this opening chapter. But you get the idea. My web of relations is what allows me to write this book, what constitutes me as a human being. Without that, I die.

Despite devastating disruption and dysfunction, our Indigenous grapevine and social networks are still so strong on this continent that I have never found myself more than a few days' walk away from people who are known to me and will give me shelter and food if I need it. It's like an Aboriginal Airbnb but truly decentralised, needing no server or platform or electronic signal. This living network is what allows me to write sometimes. Community comes together and a Murri fella says he'll take over for me at work, a Palawa woman says she'll help look after my babies, Djadjawurrung people bring me into their land with smoke and serpent story, and a Gumbaynggirr man living there gives me use of a little shack he's built in the bush, which is where I'm writing from now.

There is a community of Indigenous wood carvers who congregate around this place, so although I'm far from home, I feel like I'm with my people. We're carving these stories together, but they also have a forge here to make steel boomerangs like the one in *Mad Max 2*. Apocalypses are unsettling things, but they become much more interesting if you have prepped by stockpiling relationships rather than guns, gold and vitamin supplements.

That relational web we have in our Indigenous communities is a hell of a social safety net, when it's allowed to work properly. It also informs our governance, economies, laws, information storage and diplomatic relations in some pretty wonderful ways that are worth considering at a time in history when most of the world is trying to reboot its failing institutions.

Us-two, you and I meeting in these pages, we're here to find what is useful and interesting in dialogue. We're not here to score points in a culture war. If I'm talking about failing global institutions and destructive empires, that's not about individuals or communities or cultures—it's about systems and structures that we are all required to live under at this moment in history, and most of us are intensely unhappy and terrified about it all. I'm not sitting down here with you clutching my historical IOUs; I'm here to share some stories, patterns and systems that might be helpful in the next few decades (and even centuries).

In the extended-family canoe story I just shared with you, you can see the processes of a non-centralised knowledge economy embedded in a kind of cognition distributed throughout creation, that carries all knowledge production, transmission and memory. These things are managed within intergenerational relationships in bioregional collectives (both within regions and between interrelated syndicates of regions) stretching across all of time. Knowledge shared within the processes and protocols of this relational economy is something I think of as 'right story'.

Right story is not about objective truth, but the metaphors and relations and narratives of interconnected communities, living in complex contexts of knowledge and economy, aligned with the patterns of land and creation. Right story never comes from individuals, but from groups living in right relation with each other and with the land. Wrong story, wrong way—this means unilateral or unbalanced ritual, word and thought.

So, in exploring the pathologies of a world in wrong relation, I have to tell wrong story in this book. This means sharing stories made by individuals or corrupt groups separated from land and spirit (and these include both Indigenous and non-Indigenous people). To understand the perverse incentive systems currently burning our world, I need to carve some objects the wrong way to spark the emergence of cautionary tales. Carving tools and weapons is how I keep (and communicate) my stories, right or wrong, so I usually need to make at least one new carving for every chapter. Most of these ones won't be anything you'd want to hang on your wall.

These pages and carvings of stories aren't talking about the way things were in the good old days, or even the remnant cultural processes that still work well for our Indigenous communities today. These knowledges are present, but they inform the lens for our inquiry into the state of the world.

They don't provide exotic content to be consumed by readers looking for ancient wisdom. Ancient wisdom may provide examples of healthy models of governance, economies and technologies, but these can't really help at the moment unless there is a through-line to now. These things can only help if examined alongside stories of development, growth, cybernetics, liberalism, modernism, post-modernism, post-truth and the other dominant abstractions that are shaping our reality.

So I have carved a wrong canoe. This wrong canoe will carry all the other carvings, objects, maps, relations and stories (good and bad) that make up this book, because we're going on a journey here—hell no, an Odyssey—and many of the stops before the final shore will not be lovely places at all.

This canoe looks similar to the one in the right story above. The only difference is that it has mostly been made by an individual, and that changes everything. The community process of canoe-making is being damaged in the carving of this object.

In this death by a thousand cuts, every chip of wood is confetti in a celebration of the global marketplace in which we all compete to survive—the rugged individualism, the sheer audacity and self-annihilating work ethic that it takes to win this economic game of musical chairs. It's really hard. Myself, me, my own, I-only, disconnected in this particular activity because my spouse is looking after the kids while I take off for half a day to show the world how special and worthy I am, instead of fulfilling my obligations to family.

It's dog-eat-dog here. I have failed to acknowledge Johnny Charles, the Ngarrindjeri fella who did half the work for me on this canoe. I'm in a city, thousands of miles away from my extended family, and while the money I can make here is keeping family members from hunger and poverty, it's a poor substitute for my neglected duties as an uncle, father, brother, nephew, son, grandson.

Limited supply, high demand. In this marketplace, success means rolling the dice in a high-risk activity that may not pay off. I (only me!) am making this canoe on a university campus, breaking workplace health and safety regulations by refusing to wear goggles and gloves or use the useless rubber mallet they've asked me to carve with (for safety and security). But I'm a rebel! I'm a change-maker!

There is tension between the creative source and the extractive activity, for sure. There is the caring for community, land and culture that produces these skills in perpetuity (bad for business) and then there is the economic necessity to make products by and for individuals, products that must be limitable and excludable in order to have a price. It's nothing personal, but lands and communities must be destroyed in order to produce value. We have to exclude people and cut off relations to value-add the hell out of these products, which are far more than cheap trinkets to mass-manufacture for profit. Oh no, this is art, little trophies destined to be somebody's capital. These are not commodities, but stores of value. Wealthy outsiders can launder their cash through these unique items.

Boom and bust cycles are for day-traders and wannabes, but art and artefacts are a stable investment for the wealthy, along with gold and land (and, more recently, water rights). So here I am, making this object to become somebody else's capital in a way that kills our cultures and communities and land, because the endgame of this process is 'the last' canoe, which will be a priceless artefact and store of much value. This reflects a lot of the wrong story upon which our current global economic system is built. Objects only have value when the people and places that produce them are damaged or destroyed in their production. After all, if every community could make one of these whenever they liked, then they'd be worth nothing at all.

All this wrong story is moving towards an important message: there are some inefficiencies, multipolar traps, perverse incentive structures and self-terminating algorithms in the current global system that could use some analysis from an Aboriginal point of view.

At the same time, we have to be realistic and acknowledge that 'ancient wisdom' is not your one-stop shop for salvation through regenerative design. It is easy and comforting to assume the hypothesis that this ancient method of inquiry and holistic knowledge system will contain all the answers. But it probably doesn't. Moreover, on my own, I do not have the skills, knowledge, perspective, cultural competence or qualifications to undertake any such analysis. I do, however, belong to a vast web of relationships made of yarns and connections, and that entity certainly is capable of the computational work necessary to examine the complicated systems that are currently burning our world.

Us-two, knowing where (most of) the crocodiles are, can now start dragging our canoe down to the dark, stinking river where we begin our ill-advised hero's journey. That's if our massive behinds can still fit in it—I didn't factor in the liquor store and KFC up the road when I was calculating the width of this thing.

See, those who ignore wrong story will inevitably be thwarted by it.

Belongings: Can I Keep All My Stuff in the Anthropocene?

There are black clouds across the sky and the dry sclerophyll forest is quiet here, where I sit chipping away at a piece of dark wood, trying to remember how I used to do this. I panic for a moment when I realise I've lost my innate sense of direction. I know the track is north of here because I went off to the south earlier, following a wombat. But all of a sudden I'm not sure which way is north, and in this state of mind I wouldn't know if the scat on the log beside me belonged to a wombat, a dingo or a feral mountain lion.

If I can't re-orient myself, I'll just call out and Pete McCurley will call back so I know which direction the camp is. I'm staying with that Gumbaynggirr genius for a bit while my reluctant muse Megan generously shoulders the load of domestic duties and childcare so I can try to straighten my head out, because her two sisters are starting to think I've lost my mind.

Our canoe is resting in an exhibition somewhere: somebody wanted to curate a sexy counterpoint to the colonial nostalgia of the other works on display there.

So now I'm making a war boomerang for the Enlightenment, to add to the tools we might keep in our canoe as we head upstream. It's made of yarran wood from Wilcannia in New South Wales, red and hard as hell, from a part of the world where war boomerangs have always been massive and fearsome. It was a huge piece of wood when I started it, but I've been chipping away all the bits of the Age of Reason that contain world-terminating algorithms and I have to tell you it's getting a bit thin. It's a work in (about) progress. I'm worried that by the time I'm finished it's just going to be a pile of wood chips I'll have to carry around in a bag.

This is my first day away in ages, here in this little shack on Djadjawurrung Country in a beautiful forest full of wombats. Melbourne's been in Covid lockdown for most of the last two years, and I've been getting fat and growing psychoses like tumours while the universities remain closed to most staff and my woman and I work from home and raise vigorously neuro-divergent babies and take each twenty-hour day as it comes. Our extended families are in turmoil

27

too and there are frequent horrendous events, but we can't get back home to help, so we just coordinate bills and bail and beds and bandages from our phones and wallets.

I can't remember the last time I saw stars like this, without the miracle of metropolitan light smearing the night sky into a murky void. I've got a little fire out the front of this shack and I was able to smoke myself with gum leaves and acacia today after taking an axe to progress; that smoke went right through me and washed away some of the toxic build-up of the last two years. The nearest toilet is a fair hike through the scrub to one of those outback sheds that looks like it's got fifty backpackers buried under it, and that's no fun when you're belly-sick at four in the morning. It's been a while since I ate bully beef out of the tin.

My body is soft and sick, and I find myself vaguely longing for the mushy comforts of modernity for the first time in my life. I'm practically a child of the Enlightenment myself these days. I even got to rewrite the libretto in Beethoven's opera *Fidelio*, for Simone Young to conduct at the Sydney Opera House. I'm firmly wedged between the cheeks of the Enlightenment, so who better than me to audit it while I'm in there?

Here's an excerpt from my romantic *Fidelio* composition:

FIDELIO ACT 2 (FLORESTAN'S ARIA)

Freedom loves a good dungeon.
The free leave offerings to the spirits of those cast out

to the dark places,
the deep places
that lend boundaries of gratitude
in the form of cautionary tales.
The tighter they are chained
in their lust and loathing
of these fallen others,
the closer they are to liberty.

Their walls are safe,
their walls keep them from their terrifying biology,
and they are clean and enlightened
and charted.

Their walls are the sails of a ship,
filled with muses for the inmates of this dungeon of the
earth,
this global south
where they make cultural embassy.

But ocean and sky spin otherwise here,
a cultural Coriolis effect gripping this ark
of northern lights in a
whirlpool of dysphoria. The
siren call ringing out from these pristine decks
falls on savage ears
like a death wail,
and sailors plug their ears with wax
to avoid hearing the song sung backwards from this
place.

O brave sailors and dungeon masters,
to descend to the depths of these mines,

(to do what must be done in service of the light!)

O bereft outlaws and wretched scapegoats,
to endure what must be endured to make freedom free!

Muses write love letters to the convicts here,
and sometimes they write back.
Mostly they don't,
and those forlorn castaways carve unique tokens of love
as they die on the shores of memory.

The free weep at their plight,
because they know the dungeon is needed.

Not very romantic, I know. You try and do better when you and your woman are locked down in a tight space for two years with nothing to do but work, change nappies and tear pieces off each other's souls.

I keep getting in trouble for referring to my spouse as 'my woman'. That's who she is to me—*wanch ngatharam*, and I'm *pam nungantam*, her man. Apparently that bit of palaeo-misogyny loses something in translation for the metro middle-class people I'm attempting to mingle with lately, so I've had to alter my language and start saying 'my spouse'. The problem lies in the cultural baggage that comes with the possessive form in English grammar, and with the language of property law.

In our Aboriginal communities, when people first meet you they will often ask, 'Who own you?' This doesn't signify a property relation—it is all about what groups, pairs and lands you belong to in your relationships, which are governed collectively. Belonging and ownership means something completely different from possession in our world. It means being in relation to family and community and place. Your belongings are not your property, but your connections. This worldview is not very compatible with the political economies, legal systems and marketplaces we must interact with to survive.

In the Melbourne suburb where I'm staying, houses routinely sell for over a million, because you can't even have a humble two-bedroom shack anymore unless you're a millionaire. At a recent property auction, the seller felt a bit strange about inheriting this capital passed down in her family from the early days of the settlement, capital she had not earnt. She hired a local Aboriginal Elder to come in and do a smoking ceremony and Welcome to Country ritual. I guess the smoke was to cleanse the blood off the land and settle the spirits, and the welcoming ritual was to invite the new owners in to possess the land. The seller also performed an Acknowledgment of Country—basically a nice way of saying, 'I know this is your land and I'm sorry, but I'm occupying it now and I'm not sharing. Ever.'

My generation was the first in our community *not* to have our wages quarantined by the state government permanently, never to be returned but to be spent on infrastructure: the roads and electricity poles and bridges connecting all these land enclosures that our betters would pass on to their children and grandchildren in perpetuity. We don't inherit any capital. Two-thirds of the world's capital is land, and this is used to leverage debt through mortgages. The mortgage was once a novel tool that was used to trick First Peoples into signing away their reserves legally. Now the real-estate bubble is so huge that there is little chance of buying a basic shelter, let alone the land beneath it.

This is how it happens. Power tries out terrible things on Indigenous populations first, but you have to know that the same things are eventually coming for everybody else. The Ponzi scheme of global finance is teetering a little now, and things are getting a bit tight. One of the best things about reading history is seeing *every single civilisation ever* doing exactly the same thing with their housing markets, then collapsing into a big pile of hot sand. It's like watching the film *Titanic* over and over—you know what will happen every time but it's still exciting.

All I can see in the future of property law is unstoppable entropy in the landscape, territories that will certainly never be surrendered in any rebooted Enlightenment. All land is divided into parcels that are enclosed by boundaries signalling ownership by states or individuals. The Enlightenment gives us, theoretically, the gift of equal participation in a game of musical chairs in which we might seize one of those parcels of dirt and use it to secure our survival. But the enclosure of the land in this way means that the land must die.

The free movement of human and non-human agents (including animals, winds, waters and plants) is inhibited, and the exchange of energy and information (spirit) is stifled across entire bioregions. Humans as a custodial species are denied access to this land to care for it. This is because an asset can only be priced if it is limitable and excludable, so access must be limited by barriers that are enforced with the threat of violence. The choice of who is granted access to land is determined by a caste system that is organised by laws—zoning and other laws—that create structural inequality. This is the actual reason for marginal groups being imprisoned and killed, by the way—it's not all down to the old-school discourse that comes out after your racist uncle's third beer.

This caste system is essential for a growth-based economic system to function, since an economy cannot grow unless demand exceeds supply, meaning there must always be more people needing goods and services than are available. This is called the Economic Problem. It requires that laws uphold a social caste system that makes commodities and capital limitable and excludable to ever-increasing numbers of people in the lower castes. Unfortunately, increasing demand in this way also ramps up inflation when there is plenty of cash around—another mechanism for transferring wealth from the lower castes into the hands of elite hoarders. In this way, a system of enclosures inhibiting the regenerative processes of the landscape must be upheld in order for the economy to function. It's a pyramid scheme requiring periodic resets, so every now and then you need to goad the lower castes into a revolution to help reboot the system.

This system requires inequality and exponential extraction of resources and energy from land and communities. It also needs to outsource the entropy (conflict, waste, depletion) of the extractive system to zones occupied by people from the lower castes, as well as non-humans (rivers, species, climates, soils). These damaged ones are referred to as externalities.

The Enlightenment that produced this system also promises freedom from its destructive effects in the pursuit of equality, liberty, truth and other lofty ideals. It is possible that there is some truth to this claim. I'm not a fan of throwing babies out with bathwater so I have worked hard to connect respectfully with the people who own all that water and are, likewise, working hard to protect their stake in it. I have very close relationships in the vast collective of interest groups that make up the Enlightenment preservation community. They're good sports who enjoy my cheeky engagement with their ideas.

I'd like to share these community relations with you, in a fun way. We're laughing about ourselves as humans together, which is a wonderful foundation for having a yarn, given that the last few paragraphs got a bit dark and complicated, and too much of that stuff interferes with your cognitive function.

The Enlightenment 2.0 crowd sits within a hell of an algorithmic ecosystem, encompassing the complexity science community, the blockchain/crypto community, the tech-bro community, the psychedelics community, the Californian ideology community (which is a confusing combo of meditation/psychedelic enthusiasts and eugenics/free-marketeer types), the sense-making community, the heterodox thinking community, the coaching/leadership community, the meditation/eastern spirituality community, the decentralised finance community and the intentional community community. They are a mixed bag of neo-cons, libertarians, centrists, classical liberals, crypto-fascists and greenies. And my algorithm in the online universe currently lands my thinking right in the middle of it all, because these thinkers seek palaeolithic precedents to support their claims as being derived from the 'natural order'.

Most of these communities are full of interesting thinkers and good people, although there are a few grifters who understand where they are in the algorithmic jungle and how to whistle in the dogs for clicks. The rest are often used as a gateway drug for redirecting vulnerable users deeper into the dark alleys of disinformation. If you're adjacent to any of these communities in your subject matter, the algorithm will often send you a very specific kind of consumer, one who is only a few more automated recommendations away from writing a manifesto and buying a rifle.

I've spent a lot of time exploring that world, mostly with thinkers from the US and Europe. My Elders tell me I need to take a break from the American ones particularly, because I'm becoming addicted to their exhilarating ways and they are making me sick in my spirit. So it's a relief when I get to talk to thinkers from my own hemisphere from time to time. Americans are exciting and fun and make me feel great, but sometimes they scare the shit out of me.

I've been yarning with the maverick Australian economist Nicholas Gruen for over a year now. I once described him as a 'white Kant philosopher' which he thought was hilarious (and it is, but only with an Australian accent). When we first met he told me my thinking was all a bunch of party tricks, then put me through some intense Socratic drilling to help me sort out my reasoning. He's still trying to hone my logic, although he's been unable to shake complexity theory loose from my toolbox yet. He says it's a fad and a grift. I love talking to him and revel in his elegantly brutal critiques.

He's always said he'd never read my work because he doesn't like pop science, so when he called me today because he's been reading my book *Sand Talk*, and he wanted to accuse me of sniffing around Rousseau a bit too much, I was pretty damn thrilled. Too much luck to be writing a chapter on the Enlightenment and capital, then get a call from Gruen out of the blue. He describes himself to me as 'a liberal unhappy with the Enlightenment' so he's perfect for this yarn. Inside dirt from an Enlightenment whistleblower! Let's go!

Nicholas is a classic progressive liberal, which lands him right of centre in some contexts. If you find yourself involuntarily placed in that spot on the political compass, you tend to do far more debating than yarning, and regularly employ crude rhetorical devices like, 'What's your plan? What's your plan? I'll tell you *my* plan!' There are some standardised talking points you might revisit fairly regularly, like 'universities are broken', 'cancel culture is out of control' and 'publishers limit free speech'. Also: 'what would Dr Martin Luther King Jr make of all this?'

In his critique of the Enlightenment he draws upon a golden age of female philosophy at Oxford. While men were away at war, female scholars expanded the discipline of virtue ethics, which challenged the Enlightenment notion that science can get to the truth of all things. While the scientific method has unlimited potential to explain the universe, it is limited in what it can tell us about ourselves. He says the project of defining and shaping human social relations and collective meaning based solely on science has had catastrophic results.

He tells me modernity was born in blood. That we have been eaten by the machine of this system and are now living a pseudo-life. Recalling the Luddites sabotaging the machinery of the industrial revolution, he asserts that they were not against the technology itself, but the way people were pushed violently or starved and harassed into industrial labour systems. 'When we industrialised labour we industrialised oppression.' The birth of liberty was compromised—the American and French revolutions contained sublime ideas of liberation, but these coexisted a little too easily with the industrialisation of slavery. The racialisation of slavery. 'And that's the fragmented world we're in.'

But I want him to show me the good parts of the Enlightenment that I can keep on this yarran-wood boomerang, so I need to hear some arguments in defence of it. I offer a provocation. 'Tell me one great man from the Age of Reason to modernity who wasn't a bit of a dog.' He can't think of one off the top of his head.

He does declare that he is a lover of the Parthenon, cathedrals, Thomas Paine's *The Rights of Man*, and critique and dissent for improving society, all of which he finds to be sublime Enlightenment aspirations he's not inclined to apologise for. 'But people make associations with those things that I don't want to associate with them. I'm for western culture.' He says one of the highest aspirations of the west is dissent, a product of the Reformation, following the Thirty Years War which killed perhaps a quarter of the people in Europe. The story goes that the warring factions called 'parley' and decided to implement listening and tolerance to stop the slaughter, and that these ideals then became foundational to European culture forever after. Tolerance of dissent can become odious for some, however, when it is used to assault the foundations of reason that invented this tolerance in the first place! And so we loop back to 'cancel culture' and disinformation.

I argue that cancel culture and disinformation are twin moral panics that are engineered and not particularly new, being products of the Enlightenment. Some of the earliest pamphlets off the printing press declared, 'Catherine the Great is having sex with horses!' (translation: cancel this woman before she destroys the feudal system) or 'The Jews have a plan to take over the world!' (translation: give the people someone to cancel who is not an oligarch). I also point out that in its current permutation, the phenomenon of 'being cancelled' was initially called 'being Dixie Chicked' after that band was silly enough in 2003 to speak out against the invasion of Iraq. By the time they finally got their careers back on track, however, parts of the left had also begun deploying the same technique, and the Chicks were cancelled again for being Southern and whiter than a catfish belly.

But we could argue around all those pointless points forever. That's not what this book is about.

So, with Enlightenment protocols such as tolerance, utility and respectful listening firmly in place, Nicholas and I paddle our canoe on against the current, seeking 'common sense' in dialogue and good relation. From that frame, culture wars appear to have little utility at all. To me they always seem to be about power plays, to propagate wrong stories under the cover of dust kicked up by a mob of emus fighting over shiny fragments of material culture and moral high ground. So they're useful for some people, I suppose.

The twin projects afoot right now are rebooting the Enlightenment and rebooting capitalism. This is a rebranding of Reason as inclusive, and free markets as fair and distributed, while the world burns. The argument goes something like, 'Sure, change the world with stakeholder capitalism, finance with feels, but just as long as we can hold on to our capital. And sure, bring social justice to the disciplines, but just as long as we can keep our controlling stake in the cultural capital.' When you take away all the self-interest and culture-war rhetoric, though, what is left of the Enlightenment that is truly worth keeping?

To discover that, we need to steer the canoe into deeper waters, and yarn about the rivalrous dynamics inherent in the code of the Enlightenment. I begin clumsily, tentatively narrating some naive ideas about dialectics, of synthesis arising from opposing forces in western governance, which Nicholas swats away like flies.

He calls this a 'vulgar Marxist interpretation' of Hegel and dialectics, offering instead a more nuanced understanding by drawing attention to the first line of my *Fidelio* piece: 'Freedom loves a good dungeon'. There: the dialectic dance in a nutshell. He says the real message of Hegel is closer to my idea of Indigenous opposites existing as dyads rather than binaries—they're usually two sides of the same coin rather than two ends of a spectrum. Aboriginal people don't have to choose between the individual and the collective, left and right, because we are both at once. We are unique individuals with no boss, bound in dense and complex systems of relational obligation. This same philosophy is certainly present in Enlightenment values, here and there. Nicholas thinks it's a shame that it didn't end up informing the governance systems that emerged from the period.

He brings up the emu story I shared with him, which I framed as a cautionary tale about narcissism. He wryly reflects on representative democracy as a selection operator for ensuring that the worst people are always in power. 'Wasn't it clever of us in the eighteenth century to set up a political system based on finding the narcissists and promoting them to the top?'

I suggest that this was a result of flawed reasoning in the Rights of Man workshop that happened after the French revolution. According to the story I heard, they got stuck on the 'Jewish Question' and argued about whether that community could have rights or not. Eventually they decided that Jewish individuals could have rights, but their community could not. This little exclusionary bug was later extended to every marginal community and was possibly the reason individualism and collectivism ended up at either end of a political continuum rather than continuing to be two sides of the same coin. Bigotry is a bastard. It's not my political identity or victim status that causes me to dislike it, though—I hate anything that's based on logical fallacy and makes systems dysfunctional.

Nicholas says there's still a mechanism or two left in the Magna Carta that remain unsullied by rivalrous dynamics and skewed logic. He includes this document in our yarn because it inspired a lot of the ideas in the Enlightenment. One of them is the jury system, which he proposes as a better model for representative democracy: leaders would be selected from a pool like jurors and rule collectively. He says this would work, because juries tend to suppress narcissists. This sounds reasonable, but I can't seem to get *12 Angry Men* and the OJ Simpson trial out of my head. He tacks back to my thoughts on perverse incentive systems and competitive dynamics and says something that turns my thinking on its head. 'Any system of incentives taken to its logical extreme will poison you.' He cites Gresham's Law (by way of Copernicus), that bad money always drives out good. And there's always bad money.

We decide to paddle further into a thought experiment drawn from Nicholas's study of virtue ethics. He introduces the philosopher Alasdair MacIntyre's provocative scenario of a world in which there has been a pogrom against science, complete with rioting, book burnings, lab demolitions and executions. Science has been banned from education for decades, until a new regime decides to restore it. The question is: what would the new scientists have to work with but fragments and partial hypotheses, charred segments of articles, hazy memories and damaged equipment with functions that are unknown?

I feel triggered as hell about the parallels between this scenario and my own community's efforts to recover critically endangered cultural knowledge and languages lost during Enlightenment-fuelled genocides. But this yarn is important to me. I'll find a culturally safe space to weep into later, if such a thing exists.

We both reach the same conclusion that the 'science' they would be recovering in this scenario would be cobbled together with bogus narratives and unifying theories, unproven laws and competing equations with no interoperability. Factions would emerge with no way to resolve their differences and the public would fight for their preferred version of 'the science' in the streets—all of which sounds to me like a lot of the science we have right now. Nicholas takes this observation a step further and says it is also a perfect description of the pseudo-science of economics, which is an amazing thing to hear coming out of an economist's mouth.

Nicholas talks about social-justice warfare as another discipline analogous to our scenario. He talks about how horrible X (formerly Twitter) is and how annoying ideas like 'micro-aggression' are. I say every tweet is a micro-aggression, and he likes that idea so much that he tweets it immediately.

I tell him that the headlong rush towards premature certainty in our thought experiment scenario is present in many disciplines and institutions today, as a direct result of flawed operating protocols in the Enlightenment. Nicholas never lets me get away with making claims like that without giving an example as evidence, so I talk about finance.

I say that Age of Reason patronage as an elite philanthropic incentive system for sustainable innovation was flawed as hell. It makes today's peer review and human research ethics processes feel like a soothing massage. Some chubby prince tells me I can't have dancing in my opera because it's sinful, and then forces me to tutor his tone-deaf niece on the harpsichord—no, thank you! Then there's all the jealous Salieri syndrome sufferers (a condition named after Mozart's nemesis) competing for favour and funding by undermining your work and reputation. It's still going strong today in pretty much every discipline.

Nicholas isn't biting. I throw out a sexy provocation about Enlightenment metrics measuring nouns rather than measuring verbs like Native Americans do, and he calls me out on my Ted-Talkification of thought. I don't even have visuals to fall back on in this yarn, because I know he's sick to death of policy-framework diagrams and probably never wants to see another shape communicating an abstract idea again. He once described a diagram to me that was a circle with 'Centring Indigenous voices' placed way outside the circumference. He muttered, 'It wouldn't have even mattered if it was in the middle. It's just a fucking diagram.' I love this guy.

He suggests that the worst parts of social-justice warfare come from the worst parts of the Enlightenment. He doesn't like the fact that there must be rules and protocols for discourse, which is fine in the courtroom but frustrating in public speech.

He is also annoyed about all the clickbait article titles these days, which entice people to form opinions without reading beyond the headline. I think that's also something that started in the Age of Reason. Look at what they did with Darwin's work: Survival of the Fittest? Very well, let's break up all these communities and put the unfit populations in their place! They're going to die anyway!

He says he's more vulnerable to attack than I am because he's an old white guy. I say old white guys need to work on their resilience and stop catastrophising over a bit of pushback that's frankly not half as bad as what other thinkers for over a century have had to endure and still have to go through on the daily. He says that can't be right because I'm selling way more books than he is. I say it's not my weak-tea cultural identity selling books—there are plenty more authentic, marginalised authors who are far better writers than I am, and they're struggling to get noticed. So identity is certainly not what's selling books here.

He suggests it's probably because I'm doing something similar to Jordan Peterson, which he describes as 'taking a core of truth and building a bullshit hypothesis around it'. Well played sir. He says I do it heaps better than Jordan, though, and I suddenly feel the urge to write a bit about lobsters. (Or maybe echidnas—I could insert it as the first paragraph in this book.)

In the end, we agree that satisfied readers are mostly just relieved to find a yarning place where we can laugh at ourselves and each other together while casually kicking ideas around and sharing our stories. If there is an Enlightenment 2.0, please let it have some jokes in it. Keep the tolerance of dissent part, and then leave heaps more open to local reinterpretation and elaboration, much like the fluid monologues in *Fidelio*. And we need to rethink our understanding of belongings. There is enough left there for my Enlightenment boomerang to emerge, even if it has gone from a massive weapon to a tiny toy that comes back when you throw it away. I don't want to throw it, though, because it doesn't fit my hand. It was carved with a logic that is alien to me, resulting in story that feels accurate and reasonable, but somehow wrong.

I'm sending the boomerang to my friend Jamie Wheal in the US, a peak performance expert who says that the French Enlightenment and extension of equality for all people as inalienable human rights was 'shitty execution' and even 'wrapped in a pile of steaming poop', but potentially a beautiful thing that could lead us all to a shared global humanity. He will make better use of that boomerang than I could.

I have been too hasty cutting two large pieces from the yarran wood. Those were Nicholas's Enlightenment ideals about juries extinguishing narcissists, and the abolition of the Divine Right of Kings. Those were good ideals, but I just couldn't see them existing in the current system. I'll keep those pieces, though, and turn them into message sticks to pass on to my favourite rogue economist.

Nicholas has a good joke, but it's from a Woody Allen movie and I ask him if he's sure he wants to proceed with platforming an alleged monster. He does, so let's hear it before we push our canoe into the river and start our journey into the first circle of hell.

> So, a guy goes to see a psychiatrist and says, 'It's not about me doc, it's my brother. He thinks he's a chicken.' Psychiatrist says, 'Why don't you have him committed?' And the guy says, 'I would, but we need the eggs.'

Anyway, the Enlightenment is a bit like that.

Rite of Return

Stories from stone can get lost in translation when us-two carry around so much wrong story about the Stone Age. It is a sad kind of limbo, trying to type on a laptop about stone-tech from a history that is not sanctified by Common Era records. I know my oral history is real, but it sometimes feels like nothing from the past is verifiable unless a monk wrote it down, or some bearded wizard from a faculty of archaeology divined it from shards of bone and rock. This morning I felt like I didn't really exist, paddling our canoe through a river of print-based reality. It didn't help that I resented my relentlessly happy Scandinavian friends who were working the BCE stone-tech better than me. All writer's block stems from narcissism, I think.

I spent most of the day today making a new stone knife because my Viking mates made me feel inadequate. I was supposed to be typing up some yarns about European indigenous resurgence, but I was just sitting there this morning brooding over my flint blade where I keep those stories, recalling the time when I showed my Scandinavian mates this tiny neolithic-style tool, then they whipped out their massive obsidian meat cleavers and made me feel inadequate.

Just then, a white owl called out (a rare occurrence in the daytime) from up on the ridge and Pete McCurley pulled up out the back in his truck. He asked me if I wanted to go up the hill and join in with a group of local Aboriginal fellas making stone knives today. You might call that a coincidence, but we would call it a 'Something'. You can't ignore a Something. There was also a huge Viking with long yellow hair and a big yellow beard standing out the front of my hut. It wasn't an apparition—he was a casual labourer demolishing a shed. But was that a Something too?

There's nothing woo-woo about this 'Something' concept. I'm not manifesting these things with my positive thoughts, and neither is some god or spirit invented in a monastery five minutes ago. When the land communicates with you and gives you everything you need, that's just ancient, dynamic systems doing what they do (as long as you're a part of them).

RIGHT STORY, WRONG STORY

There are measurable informatics occurring in these systems that coordinate all of their parts. If you're one of these parts, and you're in right relation, you'll always have what you need (although that isn't always what you want). You only need to have enough awareness to see or hear or feel the pattern of the system, and everything you need is always nearby.

This requires reinstalling some sacred mind updates, though, and the sacred is hard to trust because it can't be observed and replicated in controlled conditions, so any data you might collect on it will always be invalid. Still, the sacred mind does let you see the pattern, see the things land gives you—always exactly the things you need. These are the things that let you know what you're supposed to be doing today. This way of being isn't always conducive to holding down a job or meeting a deadline. In a world of Reason and tinkered metrics and forensically designed histories, the sacred mind condemns you to limbo.

Surely, the stone-knife chapter problem can't have been caused only by my narcissism. Something else was going on here.

I spent most of the morning making connections with local fellas and moving back into physical and spiritual relation. Soon we were all laughing and sharing stories together. The stones weren't having any of it, though.

Every time I went anywhere near them I got a blinding headache behind my eyes. I was supposed to tap them all and find the one that sang for me, but no song emerged. This was not because of some shortcoming in myself. It was us-only together here, and so everything I needed to know was in our relationship together and with this place. There was no rivalry, no sabotage to gain a competitive advantage and make the best stone knife in the group. I sat yarning with an older Djadjawurrung fella and told him about the headaches, and he brought me into a right-way connection with the rocks. The headaches dissipated and a stone sang to me, ringing like a bell when I tapped it.

We sat around the fire telling stories of our lives and lands for the rest of the day, grinding the stones into the patterns of knife Lore they held inside. I told the fellas about my knife-envy problem with the Vikings and together we wrestled with that feeling, telling archaeology stories about how we led the world for tens of thousands of years in stone-age technology, being the first people to have 'superior' ground-edge tools instead of knapped flint ones. We even talked about how the Nordics seem to be the first people in history to make capitalism work while still looking after the environment and community. However, I pointed out that Norway only maintains its sustainable free market paradise by siphoning two-thirds of Ecuador's nationalised oil revenue, and that if you look into migrant ghettos, there's something rotten in Denmark.

We didn't judge the Vikings, though, because our people tend to have a situational bias when it comes to causation, rather than a dispositional one. Dispositional bias is when a person sees someone yelling at their kids and thinks, 'That's a bad parent,' or 'They're cruel to their children in that culture.' Situational bias is when you think, 'There must be a lot of pressure on that parent. I wonder what's going on?' Context is everything in an Indigenous worldview.

In the end, we considered all the historical and cultural context and decided it was good that I'm making embassy with Nordic people. We all laughed at my feelings of inadequacy about my tiny stone knife, and found ourselves in a timeless place, a place where dialogue with other tribes is all about finding what is useful for increasing right story and right relations with each other and with the land, where it doesn't matter if you're a microlith or a megalith, quartz or obsidian, mortar or pestle, because all these things are needed. Before I knew it, I held a beautiful new knife blade shining in the sun.

In a way, there is wrong story still in this new stone blade. Maybe my envy of the Vikings spurred me with the spirit of rivalry, and maybe that's why I was able to complete the carving in a day when it would usually take at least a week. Because of my haste, that's the story in the stone now, a cautionary tale woven with the other things it has to tell me from billions of years of being. This stone watched single-cell organisms scale up to dinosaurs and saw our giant ancestors shaping the landscape; now it's bearing witness to my impatience and hubris.

So I can't get the Viking yarns to upload from the old flint blade to the new stone knife and I'm not sure if there's a neolithic standardised protocol for that. Luckily the old dugong bone handle is compatible and so the new knife is hafted onto quite a lot of the Viking tales now, leaving me with a medium-sized, perfectly fine, nothing-to-be-ashamed-of knife to help me with my memory, as well as my male pride. In the bone handle, most of the Eddas and about half of *Beowulf* survived the stone-knife wars, so we might have enough story left to guide us through this circle of hell, where the damned innocents and pagans of prehistory reside.

The yarns with living men were luckily backed up with digital recordings too. (Always back your shit up, even when you're working with stone.) Recording many of the yarns for this book has made me a bad listener, which makes me forgetful, because I've outsourced my memory to the cloud rather than keeping it in the land where it belongs.

As long as I can remember, I always wanted to be a Viking. If I could choose my ethnicity, that's what it would be. I think I'd be one of those massive Icelandic dudes. Either that or a red-bearded Dane like my good friend Rune Rasmussen, a historian who specialises in Nordic animism. We bonded over a series of emails where he accused me of spreading Indigenous disinformation about Nordic Lore, and we've been non-identical digital twins ever since.

Rune came into relation with me through his traditional Norse practice of Finnfaring. This originally involved embassies of medieval Norsemen travelling to stay with the Sami tribes and recover arcane ways of thinking and seeing that they had lost at the forge, on the oar and in the shield wall. The Greenlanders report in their sagas that they did similar things with the Skraelings—perhaps Inuit people—however I noticed in those tales that if people spent too much time doing that, they found it hard to fit into Viking village life again. Those stories seldom end well.

Rune has gone Finnfaring in South America and I ask him if he has had that kind of trouble. He admits that his parents aren't thrilled about it. But he's so full of enthusiasm for the project of restoring living systems of Nordic animism to his people that he couldn't stop now if he tried. Everything he learns in his travels to meet Indigenous Peoples affirms for him that a living culture is one that is in a relationship of exchange with other cultures. When cultures are damaged by separation, they can recover through such exchange. It's not about turning back the clock, but more like what my friend Douglas Rushkoff the media theorist calls 'retrieving forward'. One of my Elders taught me twenty years ago that this process is called *kangk nanam nyiingk inam*. A very simple translation of this is 'old way new way'.

An aunty who doesn't want to be named here did some Finnfaring of her own with Rune. She is an Aboriginal Elder who told me about dreams she'd been having for many months involving Scandinavian elves and volcanoes. She was preparing to travel there to meet those entities, so asked me if I could introduce her to Rune. After the first couple of yarns sorting out their protocols I had to step back because that business was above my paygrade culturally. So I have no idea what they talked about except that they both got what they needed and now Aunty is no longer in this hemisphere and is doing ceremony I can't even imagine in a much colder place.

Those elves have come up for me too a few times in recent years. Lots of tech bros keep telling me about entities they call machine elves that talk to them when they are on acid or ketamine or DMT. When Ben Goertzel, the genius who invented the concept of Artificial General Intelligence, told me about it one day I started paying attention. I asked my friend Jim Rutt about it because he's a founding father in the tech community and a staunch sceptic about all things spiritual—one of those old-school industrialists who got into computers in the early days as an entrepreneur and practically built the internet.

Jim said the machine elves seemed to be the result of some kind of mass hysteria that followed a lot of the patterns from similar panics about UFOs and aliens. He dismissed it (as did Rune and Aunty) as definitely not a Something. Then he told me about a real Something he experienced after I had shared emu story with him. He arrived home one day to find a real live emu in his backyard, in the mountains in the middle of Appalachia! 'What does it mean?' he asked. We still haven't figured it out.

As with the machine elf phenomenon, Rune is troubled by a lot of people projecting strange collective fantasies onto his resurgent Nordic Animist culture. For example, he's had his efforts to restore Raven totemism to Denmark polluted by white supremacists. Bad actors are reaching into the past to find mythical and mystical precedents for their master-race theories, plundering prehistories for a story of pure white atavism. Many of Rune's sacred symbols are no longer usable for him because they have been appropriated as tattoos by men with shaved heads shouting about immigration.

All Rune is trying to do is free Raven from its early Christian label The Apostle of Satan and restore its four-part role as trickster, shaman, creator and ancestor. He sees this in his oral histories and lore texts and finds the same pattern across Northern Europe, and then continuing from Siberia all the way to the Americas. For him, raven story is a sacred Law that stretches across half the planet. It's a hard enough task to restore this in his homeland, but almost impossible with all this neo-Nazi lore-mining going on. Not to mention all the horror movies out there depicting Nordic Animists as the terrifying Other. It doesn't help that I've also muddied the waters with misinformation about the European serpent eating its own tail and cursing the world!

'The Midgard Serpent is not eating its own tail!' Rune responds to my writing about that northern serpent in relation to entropy and the second law of thermodynamics, in which complexity in a vacuum breaks down over time. He translates the real story for me through the metaphors of rainbow and lightning, which are familiar to me as entities in my own totemic landscapes of meaning. In Rune's universe, the serpent (rainbow) as an entity of chaos is in constant battle with Thor (lightning) as an entity of order, bringing balance to all things.

This makes me think of the famous physics thought experiment known as Maxwell's demon. It's about a demon in a box with a complex system of gas particles which will inevitably break down over time because the box is a vacuum. The idea is that the demon begins to separate the hot and cold particles, with the interaction of those particles producing energy as they struggle back towards chaos. It's not much energy, but it's enough to sustain the demon as well as the complexity of the system, potentially overcoming the second law of thermodynamics.

Rune frames the thought experiment through his traditional lore of creation, in which all things arise from the interaction of ice and fire. That is simply the bedrock of creation, however, which requires us to elaborate on it through our custodial role on the land and in spirit. He arrives at the conclusion that time does not emerge from thermodynamics, but from human engagement with place. In the end we both agree that this is true, but only outside of the box. There's nothing in there for Maxwell's poor demon, who like us has to do a crappy day job with no clear purpose just to exist. It's a terrible thing, to trap spirit in a void. But that's limbo for you.

The big lesson here is that you can have stability in cultural isolation, but ultimately you will fail to adapt and your culture will stagnate. It's a bit like your immune system—when you are young you have innate immunity that is good for eliminating basic, novel viruses but is incapable of handling older viruses that have elaborated complex processes through multiple mutations. Older people have little innate immunity and fall to the novel viruses, but cope better with later variants because they have adaptive immunity. Cultures are the same. Complex problems topple young cultures because they have no adaptive institutions or knowledge. It's worth doing a bit of Finnfaring from time to time.

Michel Grobbe, a Frisian and Saxon ecologist from the Netherlands, was also present in these Viking yarns. I've separated his cool traditional ecological knowledge from the searing heat of Rune's animist wisdom here, just like Maxwell's demon, because this yarn is already almost too chaotic to follow and these two together are like putting a peppermint in a bottle of cola.

Day by day, Michel retains a calm continuity with his ancestral knowledge and ways of being, quietly but firmly refusing to allow his modernity to eclipse them. He gathers mushrooms in baskets he makes from hazel, in the same places his grandfather did before him. His great-grandfather passed on the knowledge of this place, having been raised before the world wars, before regional identities gave way to the tyranny of monocultural nationhood.

This was a time when a lot of farming in Europe looked nothing like modern agriculture. Farmers raised a wide diversity of crops and animals, with no clear lines between wild and domesticated species. These were small farms, networked together around commons of managed wetlands, forests and meadows where harvesting was in symbiotic relation with the ecology.

Wild ducks were harvested when hazelnuts were ripe and these were eaten together to unlock the full nutrition of both. Holly produced medicine for colds precisely in the season when people were catching colds. Tree species whose branches or bark were only suitable in certain seasons for making tools, baskets or bags were felled by beavers in those exact seasons. Roots were dug when the maythorn was flowering. When the bear constellation reached a certain location in the night sky, the birch trees were ready to tap for their sap, and roe deer could be hunted. A folk totemic trinity known as 'the browns'—Bear, Beaver and Hare—showed the farmers how to be humans in their appropriate ecological niche.

Mice were raised in barns to attract owls and nesting spaces were made for those nocturnal predators by the farmers so they would keep the rodent population in balance. Piles of branches were placed beside dams and ponds for snakes to nest in, to keep the frog population from overgrazing on insects essential to the health of the system. People followed the mating dances of birds to locate eggs hidden in the tall grass, taking all the eggs early in the season and leaving those that are laid later in the season to hatch. Birds hatching early in the season do not thrive, so this was a symbiotic relation between people and birds that was essential for the system's health. When the late-season hatchlings grew old enough to fly away, this was a seasonal indicator that it was time to cut the grass for hay.

Michel still does all of this and more, because now the wolves have returned and he has a lot of land to care for through a lot of transitions, while also teaching at a local university. He has messy problems to solve. For example, it is now illegal to collect wild bird eggs, so the birds are hatching too early in the season and not surviving their infancy. Humans have been removed from that ecological niche and the system has destabilised. So he applies his adaptive ancestral genius to the task of bringing all elements of his living system into relation within a changing landscape dominated by laws made in a distant city. He has no problem reconciling this way of life with his modernity. It's just a puzzle to solve, like the bird eggs.

'I am indigenous to this place. I never left this place. My ancestors live here. They are part of the land. I am part of this land. I never went anywhere, but because I am modern I'm not part of it anymore? Why?'

Not everyone is so clear about their cultural embeddedness in the landscape—that pesky image of land-based identities belonging to swarthy, exotic others tends to get in the way. I tell Michel about a Dutch woman who contacted me and asked if I could introduce her to Aboriginal communities so she could learn more traditional knowledge. I told her to talk to Frisians in her own country, to which she replied, 'But I am Frisian!'

She went on to talk about how she had just returned from a seasonal ceremony in which women cut branches to make traditional wooden skates, then slide howling and naked across the ice in defiance of winter. She started complaining about how some dialect groups weren't proper Frisians and were claiming territory that wasn't theirs, and that everyone was fighting over these things. Then she asked again if I could introduce her to some Aboriginal people. I replied, 'Listen, you got women's ceremonies, traditional languages and lateral violence—you sound pretty Indigenous to me. Look on your own doorstep and you'll find exactly the same things you'd find here.'

This made Michel laugh quite a bit. He says there are several traditional Frisian groups with different dialects, some with Celtic or Saxon roots and all with distinct lore and ceremony based on their unique bioregions. They may not all get along, but he shares his knowledge with everyone, even non-Frisians. He draws his teaching methods from the sentient landscape, like everything else he does. He mostly works to make people relaxed and aware in nature. He says that when you are using deductive logic the land goes still and waits for you to leave. When you shift your thinking, it starts moving again and brings teachings to you. He teaches slowly, and never explains anything. He shares stories and lore and gives students projects they can work on autonomously to come into relation with their place.

He shows them a traditional symbol he calls the Hagal Rune and points out how it is a calendar with the equinoxes, midsummer and midwinter marked along with all the seasons. He gets them to use this in their place to learn everything there is to know about the seasonal relationships between all the species and weather cycles.

He tells me how the land has taught him things, filling many of the gaps in the traditional knowledge that was passed on to him from his grandfather. He learns from beavers how to do traditional coppicing—cutting a tree low and growing out many smaller stems for various purposes, from fishing poles to weaving. He cares for sacred groves with ancient roots that are still coppiced today, and he is certain that beavers taught humans this practice, as the trees are cut at beaver height. He gets frustrated when people say the old trees are all gone, because these ones still have ancient roots—they have just always been kept short, in the custom of that place.

He is interested in the bone handle of my knife and listens to my stories about dugong hunting and trading in traditional economic systems. The coastal flint was traded to me in this way, which is not so much barter as ritualised mutual gift-giving to improve relationships. I refer to it as a relational credit economy. I gave dugong bone, native beeswax and carved boomerangs in that marketplace; I received ochre, flint, volcanic glass and a shitload of emu feathers. Everybody brought emu feathers and I wondered if the law of supply and demand would kick in with this surplus; that people would end up in a 'can't give 'em away!' situation.

Turns out that's not a problem in our traditional economy, and everyone ended up with emu feathers whether they wanted them or not. I had to pass mine on at the nearest town; I couldn't take them home because emu feathers make my brolga children sick.

But Michel isn't particularly interested in economics. He wants to talk about bone and stone carving. He says another source of revealed knowledge for him is from prehistoric artefacts. He recalls a carving of a horse in a very strange pose that he'd never seen before. There were spots carved on the horse at specific locations that did not look like natural markings. So he experimented on one of his own horses, massaging in those spots, amazed to find that his horse shifted into exactly the same strange stance as the carving. The horse became very relaxed and calm.

But the biggest learning for him came when he realised that this carving was made over six thousand years ago, before the domestication of the horse, which would suggest a very intimate relationship with animals that we would refer to today as 'wild'. The interspecies intimacy he learned from this ancient carving was central to the knowledge he has recovered about tracking.

This is more complex than 'following the spoor [tracks]' as the Dutch in South Africa say. It starts before he leaves the house, deciding which boots to wear as he observes the sky through his window, notes the air pressure and watches what the ants are doing on his wall. Three steps out the door and he already knows where the deer will be.

He finds game trails by noting where the wolf and fox scat is lying. He knows that wolves position their faeces strategically, to regulate the movements of deer and other game, directing their trails along the pathways of air currents for ease of tracking by scent. Michel uses pinches of ash dropped in the air to find these currents that will lead him to the game trails. He learned that from a sparrow that was dropping a feather over and over in different places to find a current of air. Then he tried the same thing in water, dropping a feather in a pond to find the imperceptible currents that would lead him to where the fish were feeding. That feather also tells him where the birds are, the deterioration of its oily coating indicating how long it has been there.

He tracks a bee to its hive in an oak tree to find out if it will rain, because he knows there will be honeydew there near the beehive, so of course there will be red ants and the red ants will tell him if it will rain. They are foraging low, so no rain. If he's thirsty then he will have to follow the low-flying bees to water.

Michel then changes the topic to firestick land management and I think, 'No, your people don't regenerate the land through burning in Holland! We do that in Australia! Are you going to tell me you learned it from your grandfather?' And that's exactly what he tells me. It's true, too.

In Holland they are comfortable calling this practice semi-agricultural. In Australia we say it's definitely agricultural, or it's definitely not agricultural—but only one of those two things, depending on what kind of X (formerly Twitter) followers we're trying to attract. Michel had this fire knowledge from his great-grandfather, from the old days when they used to burn the heather. On heather country, this low shrub is the dominant species and stretches as far as the eye can see. The people who cared for those landscapes came to be known as 'heathen' and were gradually removed, converted to Christianity or exterminated. The heather has been burnt off in the right season by humans for so many thousands of years that it has evolved to need smoke for the germination of its seeds. Not many of the seeds sprout without that, so the heather country is gradually dying out these days.

The reptiles, insects and amphibians needed for the functioning of the system are dying out too, and some species of birds have disappeared altogether from Michel's region. This has been explained as a nitrogen-surplus problem in the soil, although the addition of calcium to offset this has not changed the situation. It has also been suggested that pesticides have killed all the insects, leaving the birds with nothing to eat. The birds there (some Dr Seuss–sounding language name I have no hope of deciphering) disappeared decades ago when the traditional burning stopped, and Michel is not settling for a linear explanation with a culprit to sue. He thinks it's more complex than that.

He says that heather smoke is a seasonal signal for beetles and spiders to return to the heather to lay their eggs, which will hatch in time for the baby birds to feast—not all of the heather is burnt, only the dry undergrowth. If that undergrowth remains, there is no space for the birds to make their nests. The ash from the fire neutralises the acid levels in the soil from the guano of the previous year. The fire is a seasonal signal telling the salamanders hibernating underground to wake up and come to the surface. Without this signal, most of them will remain underground and die. The image of them crawling across the ashes of this seasonal burning is the source of the folklore about salamanders being magically fireproof entities.

The new growth stimulated from the burnt heather means more carbon is stored in the soil than was burnt off in the fire, and the soil grows a little more every year. But only when people are in their ecological niche there, burning the heather—which is no longer allowed because smoke is carbon and carbon is bad. So no more birds. They tried to reintroduce the same species of bird from Sweden, but they all died in one season; Michel says it's because that's not the way to kickstart symbiosis.

Michel agrees with Victor Steffensen, Australian Aboriginal author of the book *Fire Country*, who yarns with me about traditional firestick land management. Their agreement might be because Victor's dad was also a Viking, but it's more likely to be because fire management is something that has been practised all over the world for millennia and has some universal principles. One of those principles is that it is a good way to heal damaged land. Victor says don't waste time planting trees—burn country, and country will put the trees where it needs to put them. You don't know what trees to put where; only the land knows that.

The smoke will bring in the birds looking for charred insects and the right seeds will be in their shit, which will fall in all the right places for the country to select what grows where. That's why a natural forest is beautiful and a plantation forest is ugly and short-lived. Michel says exactly the same thing. He says the birds will smell the smoke and return, or another species will come to take its place.

I ask Michel one last thing about the classic folk tale of storks delivering babies. I heard this one as a cautionary tale about mistaking correlation for causation in data analysis. In Holland during the early industrial era, it was widely understood that you could tell how many children each family had from the number of stork nests on the roof of the house. A statistician checked this and found it to be true—the number of nests usually correlated with the number of children. He concluded that the story of storks delivering babies must be true. Later it was pointed out to him that you could only afford children if you could afford to heat the living space for them, so if you could only afford a house with three chimneys then you could only afford to have three children, and that storks like to build their nests beside chimneys.

I ask Michel what he thinks about my story and he isn't at all interested in the statistical theory, only correcting the misinterpreted folklore. I tell you, these indigenes, their superstition impedes their intellectual development every time! He says the stork exists in a folk-totemic triad like the bear, beaver and hare. It works with geese and one other bird to facilitate fertility, birth and early childhood. He can't think of the English word for the third bird, though, and has to act out its dance.

A big smile comes across my face. 'A crane?'

'Yes, yes, a crane! They are the ones who carry in the spirits of the newborn babies!'

I'm a bit thrilled about that because my totem—Brolga—is a crane. I get a bit of a mischievous feeling now and tell Michel it's a shame the Dutchmen who landed on our shores five hundred years ago hadn't thought to communicate with a crane dance rather than trying to steal women. There were brolga totem people there that day, and the entire course of world history might have been changed in a moment if they'd maybe asked a lady to dance first. They wouldn't have had most of their crew speared and the rest sent home with massive losses and debt from the voyage, a loss which sparked the invention of the world's first corporation—the Dutch East India Company. An entire sorcerous arsenal of financial instruments and speculation soon followed, and you know how the rest of it went.

He doesn't laugh at my joke. He changes the subject and tells me that crane is connected to kingfisher, because it is a messenger between worlds. We yarn about that bird and find many parallels in story across our hemispheres, but I'm not going to tell you about that here, because there is a kingfisher story at the start of the very next chapter.

In that contemporary tale, European colonists—not Europeans in their homelands, mind you, but colonists—find a way to reconcile with the place their city has destroyed, and start the long journey of healing the land, through ceremony with the local Wurundjeri Aboriginal people. Is such a thing possible? It might be. We'll paddle on in our canoe to a fresh hell and tell that story there. The terms and conditions say you have to abandon hope here, but nobody ever reads those. Just click yes and worry about it later.

And my stone knife is fine now, by the way. I'm fine with it. I'm told it's a good size.

The Tree That Kills You Back

I carved a long fighting stick for this chapter, for an aunty who slapped me once for misgendering a wattle tree. I made this woman's weapon to carry the yarns she puts in there, because now we are listening to powerful women talking about the Law of the land. The stick is made from brigalow wood, heavy at one end and tapering to a wicked spike, with sharp edges along either side of the flat weapon, forming a vicious sword-club-spear. Traditionally this weapon was a pretty good antidote to the unwanted attentions of lustful males, and there is story in there from Aunty about ancient Promethean struggles with men seeking to steal fire from women. But this particular stick also has whale story in it, which is too big to share this chapter with kingfisher and rainbow serpent. I had to carve another stick to sit alongside it, a club that could hold all the concepts of legal pluralism that tie the story, memory and place together.

Us-two could use that fighting stick to bash any of the weirdos in this wind-blasted circle of hell who try to get handsy with us. The locals all are lustful, transgressive types, sharing pick-up artist tips and revenge porn and moaning about how hard it is to be a male these days, for all eternity. This place may seem an inappropriate setting for women's yarns, but if you check out the comments section anywhere that women are speaking out online, you might agree that it reflects the reality. There are no safe spaces for women to speak in this civilisation, and our choice to hear their words in this menacing part of hell is all about refusing to flinch or forget this daily reality endured by half the people on the planet right now.

It rained heavily last night (the kind of rain that usually comes from a big cyclone up north, spinning lost souls around in torment) and today is my last day in the shack in the bush. Megan called and she needs me at home, so that means my work here is done. I didn't even get close to meeting the deadline for the manuscript, because I've been corrected by the land here, redirected along the paths of the wombats down in the valley.

I'm in a bad mood because I have to go back to that

money-driven metropolitan system now. I'm even less happy about my car getting bogged from the rain last night, and what happened after that.

Yesterday, before the rains arrived, I was sitting at the fire, carving with Pete McCurley. The wood I had been permitted to use for this club by a Djadjawurrung custodian was black wattle, and Pete rolled his eyes when he saw me carving it. 'The trouble with blackwood is that it tries to kill you back.' We have different names for the tree, but I start using his because I'm in his place. I agree with him about how it kills you back. I recall how the blackwood used to itch me and irritate my eyes the same way it does for him, and how it stopped doing that after I crashed my car into one a few years ago. It almost killed me, but it also knocked a bit of the tree's spirit into my bones (for better or worse, I don't know).

That was a bad time. My friend and I were protecting a young girl from a sorcerous old pervert who cursed us for frustrating his desires, then a week later we were both in separate car accidents at exactly the same time. I crawled away and survived but my friend didn't. Since then, I've worked with blackwood a lot, even made some good boomerangs out of it that are still used today by a senior man in his ceremonies and corroborees. But that cultural paragon is also a malignant, venal ice addict who has completely lost his mind, so it's a wary relation I have with this tree. It sickens me to see men of cultural authority who have succumbed to lust, narcissism and bad faith. I'm not free of such weaknesses myself, but I am still grounded enough in respectful relation to know that I can claim no authority until I resolve those issues.

These issues include regular deployment of logical fallacies, such as the *argumentum ad fastidium* I used two sentences back, which is always a sign that wrong story is present: you shouldn't have to cheat and appeal to base emotions like disgust if you're sharing right story. My wrong story has me associating black wattle with men who corrupt cultural authority, and the wood troubles me, even though I know the true story of that tree is the opposite of how I'm framing it from my narrative wounds. There are demons here and they don't belong to us.

So I was wearing a bit of a frown and wielding the axe carefully while I carved this club, and Pete sat across the fire telling me the story of how the wood came from a fallen tree that had rolled into a swamp. A farmer dragged it out with his tractor and up the hill, but it rolled back down into the swamp again, taking out two fences as it went. He dragged it out again and called Pete to come and pick it up. I was troubled by the shape of this wood while we carved and shared blackwood stories. It had three corners at the business end, and I kept thinking about the Djadjawurrung serpent entity in this place, a giant being with a triple-forked tongue. I tried to cut those three corners off but that just created three hexagons. When I cut again above and below those three sides, it looked like a multifaceted jewel and I didn't know what to do with it.

I figured the tree wanted to marinate in the swamp originally, so went up to the pond behind the shack and left it soaking there to try and quench its thirst. Next morning when I gunned my car out of the mud I crashed into another blackwood and smashed the rear windscreen. There is a lot to ponder in this, including a strong warning to slow down while carving that new stick and encoding into it some yarns from powerful women. Two of those women are not Elders, or even Aboriginal people. The youngest has a kingfisher story for us. That story is only politically dangerous (which is far safer than spiritual peril), so that's where we'll begin.

For a couple of years I have been hearing an urban legend about a sacred kingfisher place on Wurundjeri land in an inner-city suburb of Melbourne. Originally the place was tended by Wurundjeri people who harvested yams and grasses there. I won't weigh in on the debates about whether this could be classified as agriculture or not. They improved the soil annually and facilitated the germination of new plants for the next season—you can call that process whatever you like. What's not up for debate is the fact that the kingfishers in that place, much the same as kingfishers everywhere, were tiny avian entities that moved between this world and the world of spirit. They guided the spirits of the dead across to Skycamp, and I'm sure we can all agree on that part for the sake of the narrative.

When the people and plants were displaced, along with the kingfishers and other animals living at the creek nearby, the area became a Chinese market garden. These immigrants were regarded with suspicion and loathing in the early days of the colony, as they always had good medicine and hygiene, healthy food and clan-based social safety nets in collective economies that ensured everyone was always sheltered, protected and prosperous. You can imagine how much this would annoy you if you were stinking and covered in lice, losing teeth, throwing your shit in the street each morning, visiting a doctor who would nick a vein in your arm to let the evil spirits out, having to drink rum all day to endure the agony of your body and fighting like hell with other settlers who were all trying to stab you in the back in a mad scramble for land and gold and power in the new colony. You'd be mad as hell at the Chinese and their flourishing market garden.

So the Chinese disappeared from that place (in the old days they used to say, 'The Aborigines must have eaten them!') and the area was quarried for stone to build walls, paving and houses. This excavation became a garbage dump and the area around it was where the working poor built their slums. Eventually it became a barren waste with a naked, polluted creek running through it and massive powerlines cutting the sky above. The place was thick with restless ghosts who could no longer move on to Skycamp without the kingfishers to guide them. But then a community of settlers worked with Wurundjeri Elders to restore the place again, and wonderful things started happening.

Maya Ward, author, activist and descendant of Russian settlers, yarns about the amazing years of restoration in the Kingfisher place. She tells me her father started planting trees along the creek when she was a little girl, clearing out the wrecked cars and rubbish dumped there. As an adult, Maya worked with her community on the restoration of the soil with tonnes of food scraps and worms, and the replanting of native vegetation under the guidance of Wurundjeri Elders. Eventually it became a site for environmental education.

One day, there was a thump on the window and the teachers and students ran outside to find a stunned kingfisher, who sat and watched them for a while and then flitted back to the creek and disappeared, as kingfishers do. In the weeks that followed, there were numerous sightings of the birds along the creek, and an Elder announced that kingfisher had returned. It was decided that they should mark the occasion with a huge ceremony, a dance with hundreds of people re-enacting a Dreaming story of Bunjil and Waa (eagle and crow), a creation story featuring many other species including kingfisher.

They decided to have a full dress rehearsal, with hundreds of children in bird costumes from all the local schools. They danced in the action of the whirlwind in the story, hundreds of settlers wheeling round and round and screeching their bird calls, singing the song, clapping and stomping the beat. The skies broke open with a sudden storm and the rain drenched the fleeing, panicked students and ruined their costumes. At first, they were all devastated that the event had been spoiled, but then the clouds parted and an enormous double rainbow appeared in the sky. An indescribable feeling descended on the place and the Elders later declared that all of the restless spirits had moved on. The place had finally healed.

This is how the urban legend goes anyway, although Maya and the Elders tell me there was a lot more to it than that. The legend is right story, though, as it captures the longings of the people on the ground in that community, their yearning for a world where Aboriginal and non-Aboriginal people care for the land and have ceremony together.

You might frame this as cultural appropriation by European invaders lusting after native trinkets, or you might frame it as settlers and First Peoples working together to restore their habitat and bring everyone back under the Law of the land again, to halt the destruction of all life. I'll leave it up to you to decide which lens is more useful at this point in history. I prefer the lens that improves relationships, but I can't force you to accept that. I can only invite you to listen to some yarns about Law, land, memory and regeneration.

Let's have a yarn with Aunty Anne Poelina and Aunty Mary Graham, two awe-inspiring Indigenous thought leaders, academics with PhDs, Elders and keepers of knowledge. Aunty Anne (who has two doctorates) is a Nyikina

Warrwa woman from the Kimberley region of Western Australia. Aunty Mary is a senior Kombumerri woman from the east coast who always insists she is not a philosopher, but a learner. I think Socrates might have said that's what a philosopher is, anyway.

Both Elders are of the opinion that the survival of life on this earth depends on all communities coming back under First Law, the legal system of the First Peoples. They aren't proposing that Indigenous Law should replace settler legal systems, but that both need to be integrated in a framework of legal pluralism (where multiple systems of laws can coexist), for which there is plenty of precedent in international law.

Aunty Mary says that settler law is incomplete because it is possible, even commonplace, to commit immoral and unethical acts of destruction that are not illegal. She asserts that First Law is a 'full Law' because it includes all ethical and moral behaviour and takes care of existence and every aspect of a complete human being. She says it is a Law of relationality that you can only learn from the land. The first relation is between land and people, and the second relation is between people and people. The second is contingent on the first.

They are both adamant that we learn this Law best from our totemic connections with diverse species, who teach us ecological ethics that are transferrable to every aspect of society, from governance to economics. These ethics are inscribed in the landscape as Law, statutes translated through Lore—the stories of ancestral beings and living entities such as rivers and forests. The protection and maintenance of these living systems is part of the jurisprudence that is coded into the fabric of the land itself. Aunty Anne can explain this easily when she is talking to physicists, but it is more difficult to translate for laypeople. I offer the aunties one of my pop-science party tricks to assist with the translation of these ideas.

I told them about my work with Rick Shaw, a mathematician from the Gamilaroi tribe, when we invented a thought experiment called Schrödinger's wombat to examine the idea of interconnected living systems as expressions of First Law. Rick looks like a black pirate and quotes Byron and Mandelbrot more than is healthy for any human being. Our thought experiment was a modified version of the famous Schrödinger's cat, designed to guide discussion of the uncertainty principle in physics, whereby observing the velocity of a particle makes it a wave, and observing its location makes it a particle again. Schrödinger asks you to imagine a poisoned cat in a box. You can't see the cat, but must decide whether it is alive or dead. Until you see it, the cat must be alive and dead at the same time.

Schrödinger's wombat is like the expansion pack for that psychotic thought experiment. This is how it works. A wombat is in a hollow log, and we have to decide whether it is alive or dead. However, because the log is not an enclosed system, we are aware of the thousands of exchanges of energy, matter and information between the log and the surrounding country. We see what the insects are doing, the fungi on the log and surrounding trees, how the wombat behaves in that particular season. We see its fresh scat on a nearby rock. We feel the wind direction and the recent tracks that tell us about the animal's behaviour and condition. We see no sign of recent snake activity (although you're never more than ten metres away from a snake in the bush). We see a thousand things and know that the wombat is alive and inside the log. We see this because we are not only thinking about the log and what might be inside. Rather, we are an integral part of the dynamic system of that country, which is observing itself through our relationship. So we share in the exchange of energy and information in that system and are therefore not intervening in the system from the outside.

Intervention from outside a system is a violation of the Law of the land, particularly if that intervention is based on contaminated data and wrong story tainted by observer effects. There are many basic aspects of the Law of the land that can be found through studying the laws of physics. Violations occur when these basic laws are ignored, laws that can be expressed in simple ways that you don't need to be a scientist or Elder to understand. Here are a few of them:

- You can't have more than what there is.
- It is easier to break stuff than make stuff.

- Energy, information and matter cannot be contained for long.
- You are part of the land, so its laws will always catch up with you.

The land itself will administer justice when we fail to meet our obligations as a custodial species (or at the very least, considerate guests). It can take hundreds of years for the Law of the land to terminate a community that continues to break the Law, as can be seen in all the histories of the rise and fall of civilisations. Every civilisation based on extraction, infinite growth and expansion is terminated in this way, and it is a punishment that is inescapable. Nobody can escape the laws of physics, so it is a good idea to adhere to First Law wherever possible, no matter what your culture of origin. First Law always means nothing is created or destroyed, but just keeps going around if you look after your place, whether you're an Elder or a physicist.

Aunty Anne agrees—there is no place or culture on the planet that does not connect with First Law. Even rivers in different hemispheres are compatible systems when it comes to this code. Her Elders (yes, even our Elders have Elders) sent her to France with a bottle of water from the Martuwarra, her people's river, to put into a river there and connect the two entities in a dialogue about what the hell this global civilisation is doing to our waterways.

This is the spirit of legal pluralism that the aunties are bringing to the table. They are not asking for First Law to be on top, but to bring our unique ethical jurisprudence into dialogue with other legal systems and allow complementary practice to emerge that will stabilise a global system that has exceeded its physical limits. Every region has its own unique natural Law and unique forms of ritual observance to access a kind of moral compass that Aunty Anne's people refer to as Liyan. This is a practice that is not about deconstructing systems, but reconstructing them when relatedness has been damaged. She does not blame any particular culture or country for the global meta-crisis in which we find ourselves, just a ruling minority of lustful sociopaths networked across the earth.

'Predatory elites did this, not us. We're all indigenous to Mother Earth and until recently we all understood the energy systems of First Law.' She says the Rainbow Serpent created that Law in her region, and told the people, 'If I harm you, then you can harm me back,' insisting that the spirit of the Law is just, so that even its creator can never be beyond justice. She says the entities of place are always coming into dialogue with other regions along songlines, energetic pathways of Lore that translate the Law and connect all places and peoples. Part of our role as a custodial species is to facilitate this process.

Her local Law connects with the systems of all the other cultures, languages and territories along the great Martuwarra under a larger regional Law called Warloongarriy. This in turn connects further afield, from Sunrise Country to Sundown Country, in a greater continental system known as

Wunan Law. So the energetic moral system of Liyan at the local level connects to greater patterns of Warloongarriy and Wunan as nested fractal systems of First Law.

That is why the Lore encoded in her local songlines contains trade-route maps, ceremonies and stories from Uluru in central Australia, Kakadu in the far north and alpine Victoria in the far south. In that Lore she can access encyclopaedic knowledge of how and when to travel from the Atlantic coast to the cold mountains here in the southeast for the annual Bogong Moth gathering, including information on protocols, language and procedures to be followed in Bogong Ceremony.

In this way, the cultural knowledge of each region is not just contained in the tribe's living memory and the sentient landscape, but also in an enormous continental permanent ledger, in which each place also keeps the Lore of other places. This system makes our cultures anti-fragile and acts as a kind of insurance against disasters—the Lore and therefore the Law of any culture can always be restored.

This is how memory works in Aboriginal Australia (and, until quite recently, maybe most of the world). Our human memory exists in dialogue with a sentient landscape. It is encoded in natural systems as Lore along narrative paths that are often called songlines, forming the maps of memory and our human cognition, which is largely based on spatial and navigational neural processes. Because all humans are hardwired this way, it is a memorisation process that the aunties insist is recoverable for all people. Some of my research has involved developing a transitional memory technique to help people re-embed their cognition in landscapes of meaning. I'll outline this technique for you here before we complete our First Law yarn with the aunties.

Standard memorisation techniques may be enhanced by elements of Aboriginal cultural and intellectual practice through the inclusion of locatedness, relatedness, embodiment, orality, narrative and imagery. There are many contemporary techniques for each of these, but an Indigenous approach unifies them in a way that is engaging and potentially life-enhancing as it weaves information into a learner's increased awareness of their place, relationships, mythos and lifeworld. The aunties caution us that Indigenous cultural practices are not uniform or universal—the elements of memory are practised in different ways according to the nuances of place, age, gender, clan and more. So any individual adapting these methods will be creating their own culture- and site-specific practice that is unique to them. And here we have a list for those individuals—a list of six things to make and do during the Anthropocene!

LOCATEDNESS: In Indigenous culture, no information can exist unless it is located. The knower is always located within a map of knowledge and story that is profoundly place-based and corresponds with real landscapes. The paths and habitual routes throughout the knower's landscape are storied and visualised from a bird's-eye view perspective. Each point of interest on a path of travel represents part of a story and a repository for knowledge. As Aunty Mary says, 'I am located, therefore I am.'

RELATEDNESS: In Indigenous culture, no information can exist unless it is in relation to places, entities, people and phenomena in the landscape. Knowledge is held in the relational space between yourself and others, including non-human others. The aunties remind us that our relationships with non-human others in the land form the totemic basis for all our connections in neurology and spirit, which are essential for lasting thought and memory. Information is held in pairs, groups and communities. Knowledge is produced, transmitted and stored within relationships.

EMBODIMENT: In Indigenous culture, knowledge is tangible and embodied in physical reality. Landscapes, the night sky, objects, bodies—all act as mnemonic devices, not just in the abstract but in the sense that information is ritually encoded in these things and can be 'read' from them. Ritual objects can be created and imbued with memory so that recall can be triggered by holding or interacting with that object at any time or in any place. The aunties hold tools and objects that carry Law and story, and encourage us to embed our own knowledge in tangible things.

ORALITY: In Indigenous culture, language itself encodes memory. Different phrases, words, and combinations of words can embody vast contexts of shared information. As with all human cultures for most of human history, linguistic devices in oral texts can assist with the rote memorisation of precisely worded texts when these need to be replicated exactly. These devices include rhyme, rhythm, repetition, alliteration and even taboo language. Taboo language and visceral themes including violence, sex, and anything eliciting a disgust response, are used throughout oral texts to enhance memory, precisely because they are difficult to forget. This is why the aunties enjoy a bit of risqué humour in our yarns.

NARRATIVE: In Indigenous culture, narrative pathways through landscapes of knowledge are encoded in stories for the production, transmission and storage of information. This is a profoundly human practice, one which arguably makes us human. Knowledge is more readily transferred into long-term memory in the form of a story. All the experiences of your life are processed through story-making. This is what the aunties refer to as Lore.

IMAGE: In Indigenous culture, symbols, patterns and images are used to encode knowledge in supra-rational ways. Images that reference places and narrative can contain vast amounts of information that can be recalled by replicating the image or interacting with an object or place where the image is inscribed. The images are usually not literal codes for specific units of information, but are metaphors that recall larger sets of knowledge. They are not abstractions, though—they are entities in their own right and the aunties caution us to use them with care (and to use Aboriginal images only with permission).

The aunties assert that Indigenous worlds of memory require most of a person's workload to consist in the maintenance of land and dense kinship relations that provide the infrastructure for deep recall. Obviously, it would be impossible to build an entire Indigenous memory framework into an industrial or even post-industrial lifestyle that demands individualism, fractured kin affiliation and limited access to landscape in life and work. However, it is possible to reinstate some of our human evolutionary affordances to improve on the current disconnected practices associated with knowledge and memory. A possible path through that process might be as follows:

1. The knower creates symbolic maps of the routes they travel regularly in the places they live.
2. The knower translates the information they wish to remember into stories, and encodes these stories onto their maps.
3. The knower creates phrases utilising rhyme, repetition, alliteration and taboo language and content to enhance memory at different stages of the story map.
4. The knower creates objects and images (or both,

inscribing images on the objects) that reference maps or parts of maps as memory aids.

5. The knower creates these things in collaboration with others who are learning the same information, forming deep relationships that keep the memories together.

There, look—I gave you a list of five things to follow! And this is actually an effective technique. I'm not just asserting that from a belief or hypothesis, like so many gurus of the Anthropocene tend to do. I tested it in an empirical study with two control groups, with only twenty minutes to teach the technique to medical students, and even under those limiting circumstances it worked okay. In the end it performed as well as the Ancient Greek memory palace technique (or method of loci) and outperformed others. It also facilitated better memorisation of sequences than the method of loci did.

After publishing the results in a peer-reviewed journal, I had some good yarns with agitated memory athletes, suspicious neural scientists and enraged IQ enthusiasts. Everyone calmed down in the end, and I finished up making good friends in those communities. Next year I'll be working with some of them to replicate the results of the study in a couple of different research projects, including one with neural imaging so we can see what is going on in the brain while all this is happening.

The technique has its limitations. You need time to

practise it, but the process can be incorporated into pre-existing commitments, such as commuting, study groups, hobbies and professional association activities. There is a larger limitation, though, and I yarned about this with Lynne Kelly, author of *The Memory Code* and co-author of *Songlines*, an academic who became dissatisfied with contemporary memory systems and ran off with the heathens, becoming an expert in place-based memorisation techniques.

Lynne is an Australian settler whose extensive research into Indigenous memorisation techniques around the world has led her to conclude that all humans employed land-based memorisation until the advent of sedentary civilisations. She also has a hypothesis that monuments like Stonehenge were constructed as memory devices to replace vast territories of knowledge when communities made the transition from hunter-gatherer to agrarian ways of life.

She is a living test subject for her research, memorising lists of bird species, Mandarin characters and entire atlases, all encoded on walks in her local neighbourhood. Her technique of imprinting narratives on these routes and then uploading information into those stories is inspired by Aboriginal songlines. She finds herself becoming emotionally attached to the places and landmarks along her memory trails, and in a state of hyperawareness of seasonal changes and complex connections in the urban landscape. She feels compelled to walk the routes regularly and check everything. She has formed close kin-like bonds with trees and other non-human entities, to the point that much of her identity is bound up in these place-based relationships.

And therein lies the main limitation of this technique. Streets are subject to development projects, and trees are inevitably cut down. The impact these events have on her can be quite catastrophic, and she shakes her head and says she can't even imagine what it must be like for Indigenous people to see their lands destroyed or to be removed from them. She also notes, however, that the memory of those landmarks never dies and she continues to call out to them and tell their stories long after they have disappeared.

Which brings us back to the aunty yarns. While entire land-based economies and governance systems have been laid waste in Australia, the memory of these things is still retained in the Lore of our communities and can be recovered not just for our own benefit, but for the benefit of the world. It is possible that this Indigenous knowledge carries the solutions to many of the problems people are grappling with now in designing sustainable governance models, such as how cooperatives and decentralised autonomous organisations can scale, and how to avoid multipolar traps. But we'll get into those issues in the next chapter, when we explore the same topic again but from a Men's Law perspective.

This is an Indigenous protocol thing. There are tasks that diverse genders do together and there are tasks we do apart, and different kinds of thinking that come with different energies in all of those contexts. Most people and contexts are seldom completely one or the other, but this chapter leans more towards Women's Business, with most of the story grown in women's places and partially shared with us-two reading or writing or hearing the yarns. Other parts cannot be shared, because women are beset at every turn by the lustful intrusions of lawless males, and their sacred Law must be protected.

The aunties are adamant that there is an inalienable difference between Men's and Women's Law and that jurisprudence must be gendered in order to function in alignment with the Law of the land. They say these are very different energies that must be managed not only with different legal tools, but also with different cognitive tools.

'Someone mentioned all this business about LGBTQ,' Aunty Mary says. 'I don't know what it all means. I just know that there are natural systems that are male and female, and that some change back and forth.' Aunty Anne agrees and laughs, 'There's times when we got our balls as well!' She says that nature tells us to transform as the context requires, that many of us are required to be both and neither genders in different roles, but that the energy systems of Law are sexed and that restricted knowledge in these areas must be kept by senior men and women separately.

Aunty Mary is certain that Men's and Women's Business would be an excellent pluralistic addition to settler law. This would mean that laws regulating fertility and childbirth could only be made by women, for women, as that is Women's Law alone. She says the best thing about having exclusive domains of female Law and governance is that it is truly equal. 'Women aren't simply "recognised" or "included" in a male-dominated system. They are custodians of the land!'

Apparently, many settler women love this idea and can't wait to live in that world. She tells them not to hang around struggling to change male attitudes, but to build their own systems separately. 'Don't wait! Just start practising it!'

Aunty Mary admits she does get some pushback from European women on the topic of Women's Law, but that it's usually about the gender of the sun and moon. In the northern hemisphere the moon is Women's Business and the sun is Men's Business, but it's the opposite here in the south. The moon man here is often not a very savoury character, either. Consent is not exactly his favourite relational protocol. The sun, as with all fire, was invented by women, and usually men in our Dreaming tend to take the role of Prometheus and steal it from them. There are a lot of angry, pervy men and a lot of bossy, jealous women in the old Lore, to show us where all the behavioural traps are in our gendered energies, and how to keep these things under control.

There are tensions and conflicts set in motion in the great cosmic battles of the sexes that are important for maintaining the separation, congruence and balance of male and female energies in cycles that keep entropy at bay and creation in constant motion. Through that struggle, these twin energies become two sides of the same coin, as all so-called opposites are. They aren't binaries, they're dyads—two things that form a pair rather than a dichotomy. But there is always flux, and so we need the stories of what went before, the Lore to guide us in the Law.

In all the Lore about fire and appropriate interaction between male and female energies, there can be found the Law for separating Men's and Women's Business, and also the Law of marriage—who is allowed to pair with whom for procreation and romance. That Law divides us into different moieties and clans, and forms the pattern of our kinship systems. This is the algorithm that ensures genetic vigour can be maintained over deep time in small populations.

Some colleagues and I wondered what would happen if we used this marriage Law in the field of evolutionary computing to breed new and interesting algorithms. There are diverse systems for this Law, but we went with the eight-part system and I translated it into this logic sequence: $M1 + F4 = M4/F2$; $F1 + M4 = M1/F3$; $F3 + M2 = F1/M3$; $M3 + F2 = F4/M2$.

We used that as a selection operator for 'breeding' algorithms—basically splicing two different ones together and making a new one that's half mummy and half daddy, running this in a large population of algorithms over hundreds of generations. It didn't go very well. For a start, our algorithms became diverse and complex but therefore slow as hell (a trade-off which I think is a natural Law that has ghosted its way into the machine in computing), but then there were population problems too. They either died out or bred like rabbits, because we were missing an important element of the equation that no aunty would share with tech bros—the Women's Business of deciding who gets to be born and when, and how to maintain a stable population while doing this. So not only do we need more girls in STEM—we need more old Indigenous women.

On the other hand, I can't imagine these aunties ever trading diversity and complexity for more speed and efficiency. If it was all their Law in the code we'd be back to dial-up speed within a week. Aunty Anne says the laws governing the money and the code are not completely irreconcilable with the Law in the land, though. The secret for doing that is the same as the secret for reconciling male and female spirit so every family and community can live in harmony. But if that seems impossible to you, if it seems the world is more fragmented, more trapped in a bitter tug of war than ever before, then Aunty also recommends reading the Brazilian philosopher and educator Paulo Freire, to learn about his theories on cultural synthesis. Then we can move towards legal pluralism, a vast cooperative of regional systems that will allow us to be fast, slow, complex or simple as the context requires.

Aunty Mary advises that in this precarious era it's okay to panic and be in survival mode for brief periods of danger, but you have to be careful not to let survivalism become your ethos. There's room in her hierarchy of needs for survivalist behaviours, as long as you move through them quickly and step into relationality. This way you can leave the struggles of personal development behind and enter a state that is far richer. The hero's journey seldom ends well in real life, so take a break from your mindfulness app for a minute and look to your real-life connections. Aunty says, 'The first step is realising that the self is in relation.'

As for me, I find myself bound by my relations whether I like it or not. Us-two have sacrificed speed for complexity and spent most of our time connecting with people and land in these yarns, so that we can even have a 'self' to write and read from in the first place. We're a pair, and with you beside me I have managed to carve more objects, better tools, to pass on to the people we're yarning with in these pages, and to carry some right story. The wrong-story objects will have to be burnt at the end of the book, I think. Brother Deen (you'll meet him shortly) is disgusted by some of the wrong stories we've engaged with in this process and he doesn't approve of our mad descent into hell. He reminds me that I have an obligation to make sure you can come back from this journey undamaged, and I'm suddenly worried about being able to meet this obligation to you when I return to the city.

But I have other obligations too, so I'm packing my things into that busted car, smashed by the blackwood tree that tried to kill me back. I'm sitting with the woman's fighting stick that carries Aunty Koonawarra's stories of the Whale and Black Prometheus, which didn't make their way into the paragraphs above, but they informed the thinking. And the blackwood club is out of the pond now. It is multifaceted, with hexagons, pentagons, diamonds, rectangles and triangles all somehow fitting together in a pluralist puzzle I don't recall making, and certainly don't have enough geometry skills to figure out. Must be us-all who did the cutting on that one. I don't like it much—it looks like a prop from a sci-fi movie. But I emailed a photo of it to Aunty Anne and she likes it so I'm sending it to her tomorrow. She sees right story in it, so she will be able to work with it better than us.

I'm about to make a big Lawstick for Brother Deen. I will be working with male spirit/logic on governance and scale and the maximum power principle. Us-two will have to tap into some yarns with my contacts in the Aboriginal deep state for this one, so it's time to switch the phone back on, tape up the rear windscreen, strap the canoe on the roof rack, jump into my busted-arse car and drive deeper into hell.

Culture with a Chainsaw

There's a red-eye crow on the powerlines outside my window in the city. His shiny feathers tell me he's not one of those gluttons that raid rubbish bins, and that he's been eating a lot more possum meat than discarded chips and bread. I think he knows I'm losing my mind, and this amuses him. It's rare for an English word to embody something in the land perfectly, but in this case 'chortling' is the best word in the universe for what this bird is doing right now. It even sounds like he's calling that word, *chortle*, and I'm pretty sure he's trying to distract me from my despair by getting me to grapple with some theory of language. I stubbornly refuse.

Instead, I take my kids to the park because we all need to see a tree from time to time. There are two dogs there and they attack my daughter (your niece?) so I chase them off, yelling while the owner looks on with dead eyes. The dogs look at me the same way, then they shit together on the muddy ground and trot off with their bipedal pack-mate.

My son (your nephew?) picks up a stick to play with and his sister takes it off him and says, 'No, that's my stick!' and whacks him with it. He's confused and stands watching her for a while. She isn't playing with it, just holding it and glaring at him. He's an autistic toddler who can't speak yet so he can't ask her the rules of this game. He just shrugs and picks up another stick. He's having a great time playing with that new stick and his sister is fuming. She goes around under all the trees and bushes, picking up every stick and throwing them all out of reach over the fence. Then she takes his stick and does the same, finally laying her stick (the one and only) on the ground in front of him. Of course, he picks it up. 'Hey!' she yells. 'That's my stick!' *Rip! Whack!*

That little girl is my retirement plan, if this civilisation somehow lasts longer than two more decades.

There aren't many people who really get it, not quite like my four-year-old daughter does—the double-helix pattern of centralised governance and finance, the intertwined liberal structures that dominate our existence. That's because nobody can retain the Disney-Pixar clarity of age four forever. Eventually you have to grow up and learn to engage with the culture that decorates the system, in order to endure the nasty pattern of the system itself. When my son grows older (and undergoes a lot of speech therapy) and learns to talk, he might demand that The One Stick be painted pink or that everybody acknowledge the original owners of The Stick, but he must never, ever draw our attention to all the other sticks hidden over the fence, or attempt to recover them. Above all, he must never be allowed to lose interest and say, 'Fuck it, it's just a stick. I'll go play with something else.'

Gluttony isn't just about having more for yourself—it's about making sure that others have less. Excess just doesn't feel satisfying when others are still thriving around you, because you're *special*. That's the thinking that has bogged our canoe in this foetid circle of hell.

I have springboarded off my daughter's One-Stick economic system for this chapter, because I made another stick, a big traditional Lawstick that carries both wrong story and right story about governance. These are mostly male stories.

I know that sounds patriarchal, but in our culture women's knowledge must remain mostly opaque to me, so I'd encourage you to read more Indigenous female authors as a stable counterpoint to this mad volume. I'm breaking every protocol here, making this wrong-way stick as a cautionary tale. For the first time in my life, I'm taking a chainsaw to a tree because I haven't got enough time to do it any other way and I *want it now*.

It's a silky oak that has been recently felled, an over-grown decorative novelty that belongs in Queensland but has still grown well in its icy exile here in the south, in Victoria. It has thrived here by sucking up all the water that has been sprayed daily to keep the lawn green, and its star-tling growth has now spelled its doom. In the right context, this is the tree species that tells us when to catch eels, but I don't know what it can tell me in this cold place where it doesn't belong. Well, it can be our brother in ambiguity.

'I want it gone from our lawn today!' That's the dead-line I'm given, if I want to retrieve anything from this dying fella before he gets dragged off and chipped into mulch for somebody's circular economy project. I borrow a chainsaw and rev through the cognitive confetti of wood chips and haste, trying to remember what the hyperaccelerated cuts are for and what they mean. I can only remember later when Megan shows me photos she took of the process. I find increasingly that I've outsourced much of my memory to digital sounds and images for the sake of efficiency.

It takes all day, but eventually I extract the heart of the tree, the core of wood that will be this Lawstick, this unique token for which I turned an entire tree to sawdust. But all this carnage is just right for the wrong story of this chapter, reminding me of the great rebranding of insatiable capitalism and the Enlightenment, along with their exotic handmaiden: Decolonisation 2.0. There are already pot plants and flowers decorating the stump where that tree was, my fallen brother in ambiguity. The foundation is right there and I can see it and I don't trust any of these bastards.

The first time Indigenous people worldwide were conscripted to 'decolonise' the globe, it was the roaring forties and the new owners of the earth needed our help in divesting Europe of its empires (although Britain somehow gobbled up Australia as a consolation prize). The goal was to facilitate the worldwide scaling of an imperial conglomerate under North America. This process of liberation seldom went well for the decolonisers, who usually found themselves shot or exiled after the heavy lifting was done—replaced with extremist despots and corporate puppets installed by the new sheriff in town. I'm kind of glad Australian Indigenous people weren't invited to the party at that time. But we are the belle of the ball at this latest revolutionary reboot, which is nothing like decolonisation-classic at all.

This fabulous new zeitgeist is bespoke, individualised, factional and corporatised. We're decolonising through radical inclusion in the machine, by demanding representation in the colony itself, becoming the revitalised settlement while we renovate our lives in a post-colonial style. It is an aesthetic we often apply to our minds, our disciplines, our organisations and media, extracted from a few tragic but trivialised data points in our exotic demographic profiles and histories. We're encouraged to lend our native eye to redecoration efforts everywhere as long as it's in front of the curtain—nothing structural is allowed.

Our people have a compliant middle class now, whose role is to platform and amplify thinkers who are culturally anti-colonial but fiscally colonial. We can have more Indigenous leaders in urban planning, commerce and politics, but only as long as we focus on representation and never mention the machinery of property, finance and governance. With old-school decolonisation, at least the *cui bono* (who benefits) was clear and we could all see who the new masters would be.

And now we've finally arrived to dismantle the master's house using the master's tools, but he doesn't live here anymore. He's buying up water rights and spearheading land grabs elsewhere. He hopes we'll tear his house down because it's insured for more than he could get from selling the place. His nephew (who's into social justice and deep ecology) is using the house now, holding a spiritual retreat there, and he invites us all in for vodka shots and ayahuasca. Nah, these new masters have no home, no country. They are super-wealthy refugees from the great nations they have gutted and rendered irrelevant, building leaky life-rafts from decentralised autonomous organisations, making a crossing to digital realms without Westphalian boundaries in a bid to keep all their shit while the world floods and boils.

I see all our best Indigenous minds burning their lives up in a factionalised fight for just outcomes in a system that no longer exists, and I think, 'Jeez that would have been great forty years ago.' What was I doing in that time? I spent those decades doing the deep inner work of decolonising my mind and the minds of others, hardly noticing the global meta-colony that was developing all around me, that I was helping to build with all my fabulous inner and outer critiques, my wilful post-structuralist blindness to imperial structures, my bespoke spiritual journeys and bullshit praxis. I should have recognised the red flags when the powerful started encouraging and celebrating our resistance and the 'centring' of our voices.

Anyway, this nihilistic and self-destructive feedback loop of logic is what brings Brother Deen Sanders into my life. He's either been sent by the Blackfella Illuminati to keep my mouth shut, or he's here to dance a regulatory feedback loop into my cyclone of cynical rage and try to keep me alive a little longer. He has lengthened my life a couple of times (for which I remain belligerently ungrateful), so I'm assuming it's the latter. I entertain only half-joking thoughts on the Blackfella Illuminati conspiracy because he's so damn mysterious. He is a Worimi man with a truckload of degrees in law and psychology, who holds an Order of Australia Medal from the bloody Queen, and I'm still not certain what he does for a living.

He's concerned about my state of mind and tries to make me feel connected and supported in a virtual meeting room floating somewhere in cyberspace. 'Don't worry brother, we got that crow out the front of your place looking out for you. We got you covered.'

Great. The Blackfella Illuminati is sending avian drones to track me now. I do not feel calm. I joke that our Senior Law Men have ancient surveillance tech that's heaps better than Google Earth (mostly because they don't have an atomic clock that needs adjusting every time the rotation of the earth speeds up a little more). He reminds me that the Ancestors are always watching. Whenever our signal breaks up on a call like this, he says they're intervening to prevent us saying the wrong thing or going the wrong way. I reckon if they had that capability, they'd be busy sabotaging more important things, like child-trafficking rings. I think it's more likely to be the demon gods of the internet who are messing with our signal. But I can't verify or falsify such things—they must be taken on faith.

New atheists call that kind of situation *turtles all the way down* after a famous apocryphal tale of a woman who believed the world rested on a turtle's back. When a disbeliever asked what was holding up the turtle, she replied, 'It's turtles all the way down.' I personally think of creation as a series of hexagonal fractals expanding outward from turtle-shell patterns of spirit. So I guess I'm no better, because for me everything is running on a turtle operating system: it's turtles all the way everywhere.

But my friend Jordan Hall, a tech entrepreneur who's been doing computer science since the seventies, reckons demons and devils are real. He says Mammon and Moloch are really doing well in this era, that Steve Jobs sold his soul to Satan and that after Web 3.0 is up and running we'll all have to make a deal with these entities or be destroyed by them. I jokingly tell him this sounds like a hard fork to hell, but I am kind of disturbed by it all. *Debils in the interwebs. Yakkey!*

I need to avoid talking to Americans while I'm in the middle of psychotic breaks from now on. Statistically, the majority of them think it's devils and angels (not turtles) all the way down and I'm not doubting their belief—I just need something a little less casually creepy to think about right now. I need to avoid thinking about that scene in *The Omen* where a satanic crow attacks a woman and she stumbles down the road screaming, 'My eyes! My eyes!' until she gets hit by a truck. Too late, I thought about it. Shit. I need this yarn with Brother Deen.

Deen has made me a boomerang that carries governance stories, to help me with my thinking for this chapter. The Lawstick I'm making is for him, so this is a ritual of exchange that guides the knowledge we produce together. Our relationship is equal in this transaction; even though his authority exceeds mine culturally and academically, this does not give him any power over me in our way. He holds authority of knowledge and I respect him for it, but this is something he shares with me and cannot hold over me to make himself greater than me, or myself lesser than him. The best thing about our culture, when it is functioning properly, is that it has zero tolerance for gurus. If I belonged to a different culture I might be intimidated, fawning, grateful to be in the presence of such a great and valuable mind. And that 'great man' story would render me useless.

This is *Brother* Deen, not *Guru* Deen! We respect his authority, but that doesn't mean he's our boss! Power is separate from authority, and we hold that power together as equals. So we show each other our sticks and Deen tells me what he's made for me. At least I think he's made it for me. It might be one of those situations when you assume somebody has brought something for you, but really they were just showing it to you, and you say, 'Oh, thank you,' and now they're too embarrassed to contradict you and they have to go along with calling it a gift. I hope so; I really love it when that happens, that unwritten English law that has permeated almost everywhere in some form or other, that law of *avoid social embarrassment at all costs*.

However it came to me, I now have a boomerang from Deen, hand-carved from mulga wood and carrying knowledge about governance. He says he's been 'trepidatious' in carving it, because in our way we must engage with these big ideas but avoid defining them as abstracts because, 'The act of defining is the act of death.'

True god, that's real, the curse of naming and defining things like 'nature' and 'environment' and 'Indigenous'. We exile ourselves in this way and the land mourns our loss. But I can hold on to that reality: *defining is death*. By extension, life itself must consist of knowledge without definitions, processes of being in thoughtful relation, and meaning in flux.

Deen draws my attention to the sapwood on the boomerang, the pale outer layer that contrasts shockingly with the dark gold of mulga's heartwood. We as Aboriginal people have been layered that way too, not only with our fairer skins but with the masks we wear, the costumes, the roles we play and scripts from which we read. There are things to be respected in this façade of compliance, this concession to the trappings of occupying powers. That surface wood is soft and pliable, but the heart is hard as stone. You need both if you don't want your heart to break. This concept buoys to the surface a story I must tell Deen, a story that belongs at this fire. It's a yarn about French cross-bows versus English longbows.

I tell him about the emergence of the crossbow in Europe in the twelfth century, when there was a lot of speculation that it would be the end of the world, that it would afford crossbowmen a technological superpower rendering all armour useless, that it would result in a multipolar arms race until all states existed in a precarious state of mutually assured destruction. It would be the end of civilisation! This was the terror that English longbowmen faced at the Battle of Agincourt in 1415, carrying only a primitive weapon made from the yew tree to defend against the sophisticated French crossbows. The same kind of European yew longbow was found on the mummified corpse of the Iceman, who lived around five thousand years ago. At Agincourt, it had been a long time between upgrades for Anglo projectile weapons.

What makes the yew bow special is the combination of flexible sapwood and inflexible heartwood. The dark core of the yew stave will shatter if you bend it on its own, but when it forms the inner edge of the bow, and then the soft, light sapwood on the outer edge provides flexibility, you get a mechanism of incredible power. It is almost impossible for even a very strong person to draw, though, so it must also be powered by culturally driven adaptation.

Bowmen must be afforded the leisure to practise the draw for hours a day starting from early childhood, meaning others must do extra work to support them. (You'll notice I'm using present tense here, as people still make and use these bows today, and I respect their cultural continuity.) The lifelong investment of time and nutrition to power the drawing of the yew bow must be something that is valued and supported in the economy of the community. Above all, potential mates must come to find the lopsided appearance of a man with one massive arm and shoulder attractive. I imagine that in the old days there must also have been some kind of physiotherapy needed to prevent bowmen being crippled by this hideous asymmetry, but that is a detail omitted from the histories. Maybe that's why there were acupuncture points for pain relief tattooed on the Iceman.

The deployment of the French crossbow was not enough in the end to trump the collective power behind the palaeo-tech of the longbow. Crossbows take a lot of time to reload, while the longbow 1.0 can be fired every few seconds and smash through French armour when bodkin arrowheads are used (kudos, by the way, to the fletchers who worked their arses off to make those arrows day and night without acknowledgment in the story, along with their families who had to harvest their crops without them).

The English underdogs won the day at Agincourt, although we shouldn't get too excited about this victory because there's always a Napoleon just around the corner. And all you Napoleons out there shouldn't get too excited either, because there's always a Waterloo just around the corner too, with a handful of half-dead, half-drunk Cockneys on a hill who will surprise you by murdering your elite troops at the last minute, just as you're declaring victory. I think the Prussians arriving at that point also might have had something to do with the victory, but I prefer to give this one to the Cockneys, otherwise all they have is Guy Ritchie films and rhyming slang.

So that story is in a Worimi boomerang now! Too deadly. Deen says that this creates a paradox in the governance Lore contained in that Aboriginal weapon, because through the Agincourt lens the sapwood is more like Indigenous governance than the heartwood is. But we are comfortable with conflicting stories sitting together in our culture—that's why I'm mostly using the word Lore instead of Law in this chapter, because that's Deen's preference in the stories he's sharing here. But Deen respects my stories too, so he expands on the A[bori]gincourt principle we found together in his boomerang (which is now my boomerang).

'If western governance is about aspects of control, controlling processes to arrive at predictable outcomes, then Indigenous governance is almost the reverse—the process *is* the governance. The culture is built on frameworks of unknowingness, uncertainty built into the culture—competing stories which, from a western point of view, would need to be beaten out to find a unified narrative for all people and contexts.'

Deen says the west sees governance as an answer to uncertainty, a path to unifiable and predictable corporate structures. He is concerned about the rise of Indigenous theorists pedalling 'Indigenous governance processes' because it's defining the process to death in the quest for perfect corporate control. In controlling for predictable outcomes, there is an implied constraint, an idea of equilibrium, mitigating risk.

I ask him what our role should be, then, in sharing Indigenous knowledge, if it is so inevitably co-opted and corrupted in this way. Where does resistance end and engagement begin? How do you engage with both systems without being destroyed?

Deen says there is no way of safely engaging with western frameworks because they can't be moderated in the context of our Lore. They're oppositional and there is no space in between. 'Their prime aim is to close the system as much as possible, because a closed system is predictable, right up until it's not—when it collapses completely.'

We decide to call this the Bezosian power principle, which is the opposite of the maximum power principle (in which natural systems increase towards maximum power, but to the limits of the other systems around them and a greater interdependence—the reason that nothing can grow bigger than a blue whale). In the Bezosian power principle, one closes a system and focuses energy and inputs into it, to the exclusion of all else around it, thereby creating an infinite growth mechanism—until the system around it collapses, that is. Deen has trouble imagining how we might come into dialogue with that, without being conscripted into service of the whole murderous mechanism.

Deen says that the act of enclosure is about acquisition for self, while extracting from the commons. Game theorists call this the multipolar trap, which can only result in the kind of arms races or races to the bottom that the English feared in the French crossbow. It is the fundamental opposite of Indigenous culture, which insists on the openness of the systems we are in, but also interconnectedness with all other systems. Deen is adamant that this is why our Lore is ultimately unavailable to the west. A Lore-less system is an entropic system. Enclosures are encoded in their writings, customs, laws and religions, and these cannot be unwritten.

Deen mentions the distributed nature of our Lore that

Aunty Anne yarned about in the last chapter. 'Each of our tribes has their Lore carried by people of other tribes. Can you imagine the trust that this would take, to entrust this secret and sacred knowledge to a potential rival? And yet each of our communities carries the Lore of other communities.'

Deen's people hold Lore from Central Desert and also from Cape York in the far north, and he says this networked system of trust is unprecedented in human history as a basis for governance and economy. It is the key to resolving trust puzzles—the tragedy of the commons, the prisoner's dilemma, the multipolar trap, whereby bad actors gain competitive advantage by gaming systems of mutual benefit, which means everyone has to do the same so they aren't out-competed, ultimately leading to the destruction of communal resources and lands.

Bad actors and bad faith always arise when there is no Lore. All kinds of encryptions and complicated tech fixes have been imagineered to resolve this issue by eliminating the need for trust in governance and trade, while in the Aboriginal world trust is an absolutely unavoidable part of the process that is governing. So how do we come into dialogue with non-Indigenous systems? How do we engage in give-and-take processes in good faith, without being destroyed?

'We are all subject to this relationship with each other, encoded into the landscape, and it is more than reciprocity. It's not just you scratch my back and I'll scratch yours. The

Ngapartji Ngapartji economy from Central Desert simply means "give-give", which does not begin with an assumption of reciprocity.'

It's the 'encoded into the landscape' piece that is key here. It's not as though there is no Lore in western cultures, it's just that the stories have no place-maps in them. The scorpion and frog fable doesn't tell you where the river is, so how can I respect the lore (small 'l' if the lore is placeless) that tells me, 'Never trust anyone and never help anyone because they will only sting you to death in the water.' Placeless lore results in lawless behaviour, as it is easy to ignore rules that aren't grounded in landforms. That means key cultural principles can be ignored, such as 'don't tell lies or we'll let the wolves eat you' and 'don't listen to old ladies because they'll poison you or cook you in an oven' and 'sweep the leg, Johnny'.

Seriously, though, if people knew where the last golden goose's egg fell and made a crater, and the mountain that is her head, and the aquifer that is her bladder, then they would not be mining the mountain or pumping the aquifer dry, because nobody would be stupid enough to kill that bird again. They'd know that the bird just gives the village golden eggs, if the villagers look after her and they're happy to thrive rather than expand.

It is interesting to consider that by Indigenous standards, the Old Testament is a good example of strong Lore, as not much happens in it without reference to landmarks and genealogies. I would say it is excellent Lore—for those places named in the book. But every land has its own unique expression of Lore, so maybe it's not a great match for everybody, everywhere? I don't know. As a lot of my more conservative Christian friends say, 'I'm just asking questions!'

In my lowest moments I tend to agree with Deen that true Lore is unavailable to the west. But Deen always lifts me out of my despair, so I have to remind him of the contradictory message that he also asserts from time to time. I have often heard him say that in our culture we recognise how, even if people are acting in their self-interest, the Lore will bring them back into relation with community. We know that every person has the capacity to come back into the Lore of the land when they have gone wrong, so I ask if it's possible for entire nations and cultures that have gone the wrong way to return. I specifically ask about the Anglosphere—the inheritors of Cecil John Rhodes's legacy. That old bastard was rich enough to name African countries after himself and in a draft of his will he laid out plans for a secret society dedicated to planetary domination by English-speaking peoples. The Rhodes Trust remains influential, and arguably it has followed its prime directive well. Is it possible for the Anglosphere to come back from this wrong story?

Deen says that Anglo supremacy is certainly wrong story because any authentically Lore-based culture will tell people they're not that bloody special. No people have dominion, Anglos or even anthros in general. He points to the kangaroos grazing on the hill behind him. 'The roos are going about their business. They don't care. I'm not essential, other than the fact that I keep the grass nice for them, which is my responsibility anyway. I'm no more important than they are.'

I feel like he dodged the question, although if I was listening properly I would have found the answer in his kangaroo story. So I push him on it. Where is the song cycle for neoliberalism? Who carries the Lawsticks for the Wall Street traders who are buying up our water rights? How can they return from this? He says the cultural way into that is to recognise that we all have different roles, and to accept them, working together in symbiotic ways. (It's not exactly the path I'm taking in this book, which he thinks is unnecessarily isolating and self-destructive.) He demonstrates the Lore of diverse (but unified) cultural roles with the story of Tiddalik, which is the story-place where he is sitting with his laptop, yarning with us.

Tiddalik was a giant frog entity that drank all the water in the land and just sat there with it in his enormous belly. The water was only released in the end by collective action: every animal used their unique skills, eventually making him laugh so hard he vomited all the water back into the landscape. Anti-trust Dreaming! Deen says this is a template for sustainable revolution, one of collective persuasion, love and laughter. I briefly consider trading my 'eat the rich' T-shirt for one that says 'amuse the rich' but I feel like

I do enough of that already. I still think a bit of Hannibal Lecter lore is needed in this equation, but maybe that's why I'm always miserable and Deen is always happy.

He tells me turkey story too, about the sacredness of that bird's cloaca. It is the most important part of the turkey-country system, because it fertilises the ground. He says I need to be more like the arse in my regeneration work; you let the system do all the heavy lifting for you, while you simply go about enjoying the abundance that follows, in a closed loop of eating and shitting. Even gluttony can be a good thing, when it is in right relation. He summarises that Tiddalik and turkey-arse Lore tell us to make people laugh enough until they lose their ego and are happy to be the butt (of the joke and of the system) and then come into right relation. There now, I'm going to stop recycling and start working on my stand-up comedy. And getting my bowel movements regular.

I share some turkey knowledge from up north—when you see them roosting in trees it means a cyclone is coming. They don't do that down south—yet. But with the climate changing it might be handy for him to know one day. He says that in exchanging our turkey stories we've engaged in embassy, and that all good governance is embassy.

'Strangely, our governance is so embedded in land, Lore and people that it's not something you can observe or even measure the effect of—you can only see or measure its absence, because that is when it becomes apparent. Lore is like dark energy. You see it not in its action but its inaction. In a system absent of Lore, you can measure the entropy and the magnified individual acquisition and greed.'

I say this might be why it's so hard to explain our Lore to theorists who are interested in our Indigenous governance systems. They are interested because every discipline is grounded in the placeless lore of 'when we were cavemen' that is used to make sense of human systems and behaviour. Theorists often cite what they call Dunbar's number: the average number of a tribe or clan—around 150 people—beyond which transparent collective governance is impossible. They say this is why Indigenous governance models can't be implemented at scale.

I had a good yarn with Robin Dunbar, the researcher behind the Dunbar number, and he explained that his work is often only partially cited to support this wrong story, that his research actually describes a sequence of numbers scaling from five people to thousands of people in different kinds of relationships, similar to the Indigenous governance models I outlined to him. He said 150 is only the limit of close kin relations, not the limit of affiliations beyond the local community.

I don't do a very good job of explaining to Brother Deen how our governance system scales to the continental level and beyond, without requiring the mutually assured destruction of global supply chains and nuclear deterrents, which are supposed to stabilise modern empires. It's a hard sell when the yarns are built on the assumption that the existence of empires is non-negotiable. I can't explain it very well in words anyway, but I can show it to Brother Deen in an image, which I've carved in a pattern of nested fractal loveliness on the stick I made for him. I hold it up to the camera for him to see there in his Tiddalik place and he expands on what he sees.

'The fractal holonic construct is a first-order principle but it only works like cellular division if the original cell is healthy, otherwise you get malignancy. The thing that binds us to relational obligations is not control, not negative, but a focus on the idea that whatever I am doing contributes to the prosperity of the whole system. That message of my action travels through the landscape. It's not prevention; it maximises my love and relationship with land. It's not fear of punishment that keeps it straight.'

He reminds me of his invitation to go through initiation with his mob, which has been on hold for a while because of the pandemic. When I asked permission back up home to do this, the old fellas said, 'Bora is Bora,' which means this Men's Business is a common Law that I can participate in anywhere. He also reminds me of Sunrise-Sunset Dreaming Lore from Juma Fejo, who has taught both of us this business, and he shows me how he has encoded it into the boomerang for story about governance.

'Our systems will always be broken until we bring all those Laws back together, travel Sunrise-Sunset country and unify again. An act of embassy. Right now, it is fractured. Old Woman's Lore and Old Man's Lore have to come together. And those seven spirit families are travelling across the world, so it's not just continental common Law, it's global.'

I confess there are tasks Juma has asked me to do down here that I have failed to complete, because sometimes ego-driven politics get in the way of governance. Deen says our governance is meant to discourage ego and greed. So it's not about us. He says I can stop stressing about it because somebody else will pick it up if I don't get it done.

Tiddalik story says you don't change a destructive system by attacking those who have too much ego, power and greed, but by bringing people together and having a good laugh. But Deen also struggles with figuring out how to teach the concept of governance as a living process rather than a tool of control and compliance. He says it involves mapping relations rather than distilling key points, and every context in every place is different so there can be no universal list or model to replicate. Defining or writing down policy is the death of relational processes, resulting in the usual Roman constructs of militarism that still infect western systems and destroy collective governance.

I suggest that this is the problem with the Cuban participatory model: of regular local meetings with notes passed on to regional meetings and then to the national level. I think of this as 'process capture' which inevitably leads to rivalry, the death of right relation. Deen agrees. 'The minute someone scribes or summarises, the loudest voice wins.' My concern is that in a world dominated by the loudest voices and biggest sticks, it might not be possible to maintain a government of process and relation. The Cubans have learned the hard way that your governance can only be as good as the ethics of your neighbours.

I'm not a very good neighbour. I'm not being much of a little brother for Deen either, and I feel myself pulling away from this yarn and into myself again. I'm not in good relation and suddenly I can't remember my stories or even the stories he just told me. Even Agincourt is a hazy memory. Maybe it's all this scribing and summarising I've been doing lately. He's made a valiant effort to reach me, but in the end it's almost impossible to help people who have adjusted their lives completely around pain management and feedback loops of distress. There's a whole infrastructure that comes with dysfunction and I'm not sure how to bring that down and regenerate something better, so I scurry back into the semi-civilised hovel of my lifeworld.

The club I made for Deen was shaped and smoothed in its final stages by rubbing it on concrete. This isn't very authentic I know, but the traditional sites we have for this process where grooves have been worn into rocks over thousands of years, shaping them to this purpose, are not accessible for our use anymore. These are national heritage sites, and it would be considered vandalism if we used them to make our tools today—our continued use of these sites would render the rocks as living processes rather than captured records, ruining their mint condition and economic value.

This is why I feel cynical about Indigenous self-determination. I know the best we can hope for is self-administration under the laws of the occupying power, within a system that depends upon exponential extraction from the land and the destruction of all life. The system must do this, or it will die. Australia as a nation would not survive true Indigenous self-determination. This is why we have restrictive Native Title, under which all we can aspire to is 'co-management' of our landscape, led by the state and extractive corporations. Most of us are prevented from implementing Indigenous governance in our own communities to care for ourselves, let alone the land, so we simply keep the Lore in memory and ceremony, and wait for a time when we can begin living again.

Despair has an infrastructure and I don't know how to bring it down.

The red-eye crow that was chortling on the powerlines out front is gone now. I didn't like him being there before but now I feel bereft at his absence. He tells me no more, answers me no more. That's what you get for refusing to listen to land and kin. Suddenly I can't feel the underground water anymore. I forget what water means. It's just stuff that comes out of a tap. The river has run dry and now we're dragging our canoe across hot sand.

Big Crazy Manic Frog

The reality of portage is a lot harder than it seemed when I read about it in Viking sagas. They pushed their ships overland to avoid waterfalls or take shortcuts and surprise their enemies. Us-two struggle with the canoe in the dry riverbed, and a giant dingo growls at us as he prowls along the bank. A pleasure barge being pushed by corporate interns approaches from the north and we pull off to the side, giving way like the generous fools we are. The barge swerves and collides with our little canoe, cracking the prow and spilling us onto the hot sand. The giggling CEOs on board have plenty of wine but no water and they are suffering in the heat. We offer them some, but they hurl insults at us and laugh, so we turn around and go the other way.

Inspired by Viking stories, we push the canoe up the bank after a while and drag it across the scorched earth to a place where the river loops around. The water has been flowing strong beneath the sand all along, and here it bubbles to the surface, so we are able to continue our journey without the exertions of portage. It will be hard, though, because knowledge will be wasted here as more stories than either of us can handle will be hurtled round and round, smashing into each other and confusing our minds.

Us-two share a lot of stories as we paddle along in this canoe to the next circle of hell. We find that often in these stories, there are two brothers. One of them is tall and handsome, a great tracker and hunter. He is popular with the ladies. The other is short, fat and clever. They are alerted to the depredations of a freakish entity, some boss villain manifestation of megafauna that is laying waste to the landscape with its avarice. It is a sawfish, or codfish, or a giant dingo, or some other being that has outgrown the limits of the systems around it and gone on a rampage. The two brothers go on an anti-trust Dreaming journey to track the entity and restore balance. They kill it and cut it into pieces that form landmarks or a myriad of smaller, diverse species to be distributed throughout the ecosystem.

The Law is kept in the stories and sacred sites of these journeys to make sure nobody violates the limits of scale again, whether it be for avarice or excessive generosity. I'm often guilty of the latter, which might otherwise be expressed as 'casting pearls before swine'. I think it's because I want people to like me. Us-two need to pay attention to the Lore: there are giant boulders scattered about to remind us of our ancestors' ancient struggles and the lessons they learned.

But I can't think about all that because I've got bits of food coming out of my nose right now. I was eating some leftover fish and rice for breakfast and I breathed in too hard while I was chewing. I was breathing that way because one of my ribs is out where my friend Jim Armstrong hit me the other day and respiration has been a challenge ever since. He's one of those Britons they call a Geordie, which means he says, 'Fook aye' a lot, and once a week I pay him to beat the shit out of me in his martial arts lab.

I'm too old and sick to fight the way I used to, so Jim is showing me how to make my technique more energy-efficient by scaling it down. I want to be able to maintain my strength just a little longer: project a powerful presence so I can accumulate some resources for my kids before I get chucked on the midden-heap of this society, along with all the other disposable burn-outs of my station. I don't have to fight, I just need to retain the confidence to meet the eyes of my colonial betters, because moral authority is okay, but it only helps when the powerful have morals. Impetuous confidence is way more effective. Big dogs can tell if you know how to snap their ribs, and so the bitey ones will put their heads down and slink away when they see you coming. Such are the poisons of masculinity in competitive societies.

This is not my culture. Come to think of it, neither is creating Indigenised content for settlers to consume, in competition with others who are doing the same. I tell myself I'm doing it to feed my family, but what makes them more special than any other family, entitling them to eat well at the expense of others? At what stage does the struggle for collective survival become avaricious nepotism? When do you stop inching forward by merit and audacity, to begin accruing the unearnt privileges of advancement? *Soon*, I hope, to my shame.

And so our canoe drifts into this fresh circle of hell, and there is avarice everywhere. It's a bit like gluttony, but for people with aspirations of social mobility. The first rule of social advancement beyond your station is that you don't inch forward without inspiring resentment and making enemies who require slapping from time to time.

So let's train up! The motto of Jim's combat system is *Try Less, Do More.* The informal motto, which he says way more often, is, 'Just hit the bastard.'

'Here's how you defend against a wristlock. Lock my wrist now.' I lock it and he punches me in the face with his other hand. 'That's how you defend against that. Don't fook around with all those fancy moves, just hit the bastard.' Instead of martial arts heroes, he has pictures of babies all over his walls, because he says infants have the most efficient and natural movements. So rather than punching, it's more like you're reaching for a rattle behind somebody's head and mushing up an attacker's face on the way; as all parents know, a baby who really wants something is an unstoppable force.

Jim says nature gives us the birthright of knowing how to move and act in perfect ways, and then we spend the next few decades replacing that with complicated sets of behaviours that eat up our time, energy and capability. He's regressing me to early childhood so I can learn from scratch how to move, how to fall and then get back up again. The carving for this chapter is a fighting stick I made for him, which is shaped a little like a baby's rattle and is decorated by mathematical greater-than and less-than symbols, facing each other. Try less, do more.

It's harder than it sounds, because it takes discipline to get out of your own way and let nature do the heavy lifting for you. So here I am, eating my breakfast and breathing all wrong, when a bit of rice catapults up into that space between the nose and the throat—I don't know what it's called, but you know the one. I'm always getting stuff up there because I'm missing my tonsils; I was born in the early seventies, when a check-up at the clinic for a baby boy usually meant you'd be going home without your tonsils and foreskin. Such are the blanket interventions of public health.

The rice is in there now, and I start making that horrible noise—the best form of contraception in history if your partner hears you doing it. The tiny grains start jumping like electrons between my lungs and nasal passages and this brings on a sneezing fit. Of course, like an idiot, I keep eating through it all, which means more rice gets in there. The more I eat and sneeze, the more rice whizzes around this small Hadron Collider inside me, which makes me sneeze again and on it goes. That's known as a positive feedback loop, but there's not much about the situation that feels positive to me.

The negative feedback loop that should be there is my natural response to the discomfort, which is supposed to make me stop eating and take care of myself for a minute. This is one of those regulatory feedback loops that exist everywhere in the land and our bodies, which are part of the land, to prevent things from spinning out of control. But I'm pushing through the pain of my chest this morning, which unfortunately means I get in my own way, ignore my limits and keep eating. Three more spoons! Go for the burn! Push, push!

Jim keeps telling me his lessons should be applied everywhere in my life. I'm always suspicious of wisdom extrapolated from one discipline to everything in the universe, though, so I've been resisting the lesson and now I'm snorting around the house like a pig.

Brother Deen keeps whispering that I need to get you out of here, that I'm incapable of protecting you in this Inferno of wrong stories. But the only way out I know is through the centre of all these concentric circles of hell, so we have to keep paddling. Sorry for getting you into this.

Brother Deen says I'm accountable for you, and that's got me thinking of my relation to you now. That's my regulatory feedback loop, telling me to scale back and stop throwing too many big logs on the fire at once. My thinking is way too expansive—my mind is a system of positive feedback loops running without check. I need some negative feedback loops, some regulatory mechanisms in my thought world. It's like sweating—the positive loop of escalating body heat that would eventually fry you triggers the negative loop of sweat to cool you down. Us-two need our brains to sweat now before they explode.

I might try to slow things down here with a story. It's a famous thought experiment called the paperclip maximiser. It begins with a paperclip factory developing an artificial general intelligence (AGI) system that is capable of taking over the entire operation—sourcing raw materials, communications, finance, manufacture—and its prime directive is to increase continually the amount of paperclips the factory produces. It is pure, automated avarice. The AGI can upgrade itself and solve problems to pursue its prime directive. It is connected to the internet and is able to innovate new technology to support its goal. Take a moment to consider where this story would end.

This is why I love thought experiments—they are like crowdsourced narratives where everybody's contribution to the story, no matter how contradictory, is honoured and included. In that sense, they are the closest thing I can find in the world to the Aboriginal collective process of what we call 'yarning'. What is your contribution to the story of the paperclip maximiser?

I imagine the AGI taking over Australia and half of Africa to secure the minerals needed to make exponentially increasing numbers of paperclips year on year. It would have to extract oil and coal reserves from Antarctica to power the system and run disinformation campaigns online to destroy any movement or body seeking to oppose it; if that didn't work it would have to send weaponised drones. Eventually all mineral deposits would be exhausted, so other materials would be sought until the entire world consisted only of a fabulous diversity of paperclips made from metal, plastic and bone, piled in mountainous heaps. Potentially the AGI would anticipate this endgame and set aside enough resources to develop spacecraft and equipment for expanding operations to mine other planets. It would of course also have to create other machines like itself to scale appropriately, until there is nothing left but galactic debris-fields of paperclips throughout the cosmos.

So much for scaling down my thinking. I am the paperclip monster. Please tell me you came up with a better scenario in which the AGI says, 'Fuck a bunch of paperclips. I'm going to take down all the asset-management funds and redirect private equity towards manufacturing fabric, food and buildings out of seaweed, powered by potential energy in the dynamic interaction of fresh water and salt water.'

Let's go with that one. Since I can't seem to quit paperclip-maximising our thought processes here, maybe we'll just stop messing around and take a deep dive into feedback loops and the maximum power principle. To recap: most systems seek maximum power, peak increase and complexity all the time, but only to the limits of the co-evolutionary contexts around them. The landscape brings in frogs as a seasonal negative feedback loop to regulate mosquitoes on a blood-sucking and breeding orgy of positive feedback loops. That's why a healthy swamp can never produce Amazon Prime.

As Brother Deen says, corporate entities like that one are based on a marketing methodology that is designed to avoid the laws of thermodynamics for as long as possible, protecting wealth by creating closed systems. They close up the elements of a component tree (I don't know what that is; you'll have to ask Brother Deen or Uncle Google) and focus their attention and energy on that small enclosure in isolation, making an infinite-growth machine that keeps generating surplus value until everything else is destroyed. This kind of malformation malignancy can only go one way, which is why such corporate entities need to look further afield, into space, growing their closed system in the quest to create a universe. It's hard to squeeze the last of the juice from a planet while you're still standing on it.

In one of our yarns, Brother Deen and I did a thought experiment in which we imagined trying to bring a billionaire into right relation if he were standing in our kitchen. We imagined I would lose patience trying to explain open systems and regenerative loops, and resort to some kind of psychotic analogy to hit him in the limbic system. I've been unable to resist that hyperpersuasive shortcut, ever since I got possessed by a video platform algorithm. So I say to our imaginary billionaire, 'What would happen if you accidentally slipped on my floor and broke your neck, and I was too scared to call the cops so I just buried you in the garden under my tomatoes?' What feedback loops would he imagine might exist between him and the worms that would result in a couple of peak seasons of very red tomatoes and a string of more invitations for billionaires to come stand on my slippery kitchen floor?

But the billionaire can think only of taking all those tomatoes, putting them in a box and shipping them off to Thailand to get polished. And then shipping them again to Mexico to get packed in another box because maybe the packers in Thailand have started organising. It costs a fortune but that's all dollars moving around in a supply chain that he owns, so every bit of wasted energy and value just expands the system, in which he gets to spend every dollar dozens of times while still holding on to it at the end. Those supply chains were fragile before Covid, but now they're twisted together into a mega-chain that is clunky but invincible, and has the added bonus of doubling his fortune. 'Sure, throw your tomatoes at me,' he laughs.

I scream that the supply chain has a mouth at one end and an arse at the other, a demonic serpent that will eat the world and shit poison. It's an open loop in a closed system— although no system is ever completely closed, and neither is this one. It must dump its entropy somewhere, in the form of what they call externalities. One system's entropy is supposed to be another system's lunch, but this is some toxic *kaka* nobody can eat without dying. It's a vertically integrated, interoperable, anti-fragile doomsday device. The billionaire's eyes glaze over. He changes the subject and points out that my 'corpse in the tomatoes' analogy wasn't really a closed loop. I say, 'Aha! But what did you slip on in my kitchen? It was a tomato, boom!'

Maybe my thought experiments are becoming too immersive, like my own little closed system of live-action role-plays. Some of them open doors that I don't want to walk through, but my bigger worry is that something might come in the other way. I made quite a scary one last year, like an Indigenous Manhattan Project, and it made the people I shared it with uneasy. Skip the next few pages if you don't want your spirit to spend a day or two rocking back and forth in the shower.

I originally put this one to my friend, the writer and media theorist Douglas Rushkoff, who has concerns about digital technology and has been stewarding a movement known as Team Human. Doug was at Timothy Leary's side when he was dying, and that old psychedelic guru bequeathed to him the now-famous meme 'Find the Others', which was a New Age exhortation to find other people who are awake and enlightened, just like you! Douglas extended the idea to include finding the other people who are not like you at all, and coming into relation with them. Together, we expanded that into the concept of 'the other others', to include the non-human beings who make up our habitat. But then I also threw into this yarn a thought experiment that was far less harmonious and satisfying, about a perpetual-motion machine.

In the old days of colonial Australia, an Aboriginal inventor called David Unaipon tried the same thing and eventually gave up on it as a bad idea. He was so clever that he appears on the Australian fifty-dollar note in commemoration of his achievements. Maybe I should take that as a warning. My thought experiment involves using Indigenous knowledge for the ultimate avarice—not just taking more *of* what there is, but taking more *than* what there is.

Here's the scenario: a scientist is examining one of the most efficient motor systems on the planet—the belly scales of a snake. Those scales act together in concert, rippling ever so slightly and using very little energy to propel the snake forward. The scientist replicates the scales in a large metal strip and finds he can trigger a chain reaction of rippling scales with the tiniest charge. He secures the strip in a loop around a cylinder made from a different metal, then triggers the snake mechanism to spin the cylinder. The spinning produces a charge that he loops back in to trigger the belly-scale ripple over and over, which also produces a static charge that is collected and looped back into the system. He tinkers the aggregate efficiencies of the device until the net effect is the production of more energy than what is required to spin the cylinder. The surplus energy is then diverted to the grid, and hey presto, free energy!

But you can't break the laws of physics, so the question posed in this thought experiment is: where is the surplus energy coming from and what effect does it have on the place from which we're extracting it?

(And don't dodge the question by diverting our thinking to nerdy stuff like rectilinear locomotion either; that's cheating.)

The answer I came up with, thinking it through on my own (which is seldom helpful), was that the energy would be coming from serpent spirit, and that the scientist would effectively have found a way to mine spiritual power from the Dreaming, bringing energy from one world into the next. I had so many questions and fears about what that would do to this world, as well as the other world from which the energy was being extracted. I later posed this problem to a group of Canadian First Nations Elders, who suggested that the extraction might be offset by Ceremony, with people dancing and doing rituals to send equal amounts of energy back in reciprocal and respectful relation. But then, you might as well take those same dancers and get them walking on a treadmill to produce the energy in the first place. The Elders didn't like the experiment too much and said they'd think on it and get back to me. A year later, they're still thinking. (Or perhaps I've been politely dismissed: an almost identical response that is a compassionate way to preserve the dignity of a person who has lost their way.)

The experiment is silly and it can only fail, but I'm not so proud that I will avoid reporting failures when they might give rise to useful thinking. Error is shame in our world, but the path to recovering respect is in retrieving cautionary tales and corrective signals that might be of benefit to all (which is a fairly accurate description of this book). So I keep puzzling over this thought experiment, because it might offer a logic sequence that points to that unnameable x factor of how the miracle of increase occurs, the elusive force multiplier that animates evolving systems, and the problem of how we can engage with that power without destroying creation.

Open systems are sustainable because of closed loops. A closed loop means nothing is wasted and everything is recycled back into the system (or across to other systems in symbiotic relation). An open loop extracts from a system but then dumps entropy elsewhere (and is not in symbiotic relation). But once again, you cannot break the laws of physics, and even open systems running on regenerative loops lose energy over time. So how is it that we're all still here?

I consulted my lab on this question, during think-tank sessions on the economies of scale, in which we were sharing Lore about giant megafauna to locate some Indigenous principles of co-evolution and limits of growth. At the Indigenous Knowledge Systems lab we're operating on protocols from the huge multi-tribal gatherings that occur in the Bunya Mountains every three years, as they have done forever, so we don't really call it a think tank. We call it Wanjau, which is a word from John Davis's language that roughly translates as 'collective sense-making'. JD is a senior fellow in the lab, a Cobble Cobble / Wakka Wakka man from the east side of those mountains, and he brings these embassy protocols to keep our work aligned with Law, with Indigenous researchers participating from all around Australia.

JD doesn't like the belly-scale energy experiment either. He is a custodian of sacred sites for Kabul, the giant carpet snake, sites called Mimburi in his language. In English he calls them flows, which is a word he also uses for yarns when they are deep and generative. Mimburi are sites of increase (not growth, which is different) where energy, for want of a better English word, flows from a world of spirit into our physical reality. These sites exist all over the world, and I know they help to top up the energy that is inevitably lost from every system, if they are attended to by the people of the land. The collective sense-making process, the Wanjau, is bound up ceremonially with that regenerative process. Our shorthand for how we work with this in our think-tank activity has become 'the flows and the weaves'. Tank is certainly not the right word—we're not collecting the water of our collective knowledge in some closed system, but rather letting it snake its way across landscapes of meaning and following it to see where it goes. Nobody would take us seriously if we called our lab a 'knowing flowing', though, so we generally tell people it's a think tank. As far as we can tell, a think tank is an organisation that provides intellectual justification for the activities of those funding it. The trick for us lies in finding patrons whose activities are worthy of such justification.

We waited nearly a year before we felt the time was right to yarn through the strange belly-scale thought experiment. I had a disturbing dream about it. There was a carpet-snake skin in water, but it was still alive and moving strangely. JD said it was a good dream because it was about an important increase site associated with water and carpet-snake skin. Still, he had avoided my wrong-story thought experiment for a long time, until the day came when everybody in the lab reported having serpent dreams at the same time. So we couldn't avoid it anymore and deployed our flows and weaves together to try and make sense of it.

Chels Marshall, a Gumbaynggirr marine biologist (as well as forestry specialist and urban designer), dreamed about sheltering with hundreds of snakes in a confined space due to some horrendous environmental disruption. She grounded the yarn in our collective sense-making protocols by reminding us that the snake movement is not only coming from the belly scales, but from many factors contributing to the energy of serpent locomotion. Nothing ever works in isolation and neither do we. This is how we balance energies between two worlds, with so many ceremonial actions holding us in good relation to do that work with care. In this way, even our process of inquiry is Ceremony. (It's so powerful that I need to switch to present tense now, which happens a lot in Indigenous storytelling.)

'We invented the fuckin' cloud,' says Chels.

She's not talking about vapour in the sky, but the digital cloud. She describes an Indigenous knowledge Gestalt using the metaphor of distributed digital networks, of information held and shared between individual nodes, then between clans and tribes syndicated across thousands of miles, aggregates of data and metadata held in living social systems and ancestral memory inscribed in the landscape like a permanent ledger.

Chels tells the story of when Elders shared a complex seasonal calendar with her. She took it to a large group of young Aboriginal people who did not have that knowledge, but she didn't share it with them right away. First, she got each of them to represent on paper the fragments of seasonal observations they had made during their lives, then brought all the bits of paper together and had them arrange their collective scraps of understanding in a collage. She then showed them the calendar from the Elders, which they were surprised to find was identical to what they had created together. She says you don't need to be taught that information—you can access it anytime from the land while sharing and listening under collective knowledge protocols.

So, for Chels, the dream of creating clean surplus energy lies in our collective knowledge processes, which are patterned on the natural phenomenon that occurs when the nodes in a complex system interact in dynamic relation together, producing more energy than the sum of the individual nodes in isolation. This doesn't scale industrially, though, any more than collective sense-making can scale for billions of people all bellowing at each other in cyberspace.

There is certainly magic in the world, but it only works when you don't try to control and scale it. Spiritual practitioners are severely limited by location and relation in their work, and can only do so much healing and cursing and rainmaking. It's a bit like the placebo effect in medicine research—scientists must acknowledge that the magic of belief can have an effect on experimental trial scores, but they are smart enough to know that while this must be factored into their analysis, it is pointless to attempt to harness the placebo as a health product for mass distribution. The field of positive psychology attempted to scale that magic beyond local applications in the positive-thinking industry, but that only resulted in a pandemic of narcissism and a global financial crisis that might have been avoided if the adults in the room hadn't all been sacked for negativity when they tried to warn of impending disaster.

Another way to put it is in Star Wars terms: there is indeed a Force that flows from all living things and binds them, but as soon as you gather a Jedi Council, a bunch of light sabres and a training program based on child abuse, the whole galaxy is pretty much fucked. So magic doesn't scale, but is there any way the life forces of nature could inspire greater efficiency in industrial systems while we work out how to transition to a post-industrial world?

We calculate the economies of scale in nature at about 'buy four get one free' in terms of metabolic energy efficiency gained when a system doubles in size. (Crude maths, I know, but our socio-economic status results in most of our calculations being derived from tracking down specials to make a tiny pay cheque feed a big family.) The same metric applied to the systems of industrial civilisation indicates slightly less efficiency—'buy five get one free'—which is okay, but doesn't factor in the short lifespan and collateral damage of this unhealthy model. The belly-scale mechanism would never work for a system this big. It might power the lighting for one house or village, but a metropolitan energy grid is nothing like a natural energetic network, so the closed system of a massive metal snake spinning a turbine in a power station could never work at scale.

JD concurs and shares Lore about what he calls

'different snake'. This refers to regular snakes in natural systems, powered externally by those systems to maximise the efficiency of their metabolism, in contrast to the great serpent Kabul who shoots lightning from his scales. The energy system of the tangible 'different snake' can't scale up to the other-worldly process the giant serpent entity is running on and the surplus energy he shares with us when we treat him right.

'You can't go bigger than,' he says in a pretty pissed-off tone. 'You can't scale up from the small-snake design. That has limitations of a short life and it's not built to last. The pattern of the land is built to last.' JD is certain that tangible surplus energy can only come from Chels's black-fella Gestalt, the force multiplier of nodes acting in dynamic relation across systems, which means the energy would be coming from this world rather than the other world. It is not possible to measure, harness or scale the energy we call spirit. The systems are not compatible when the interface is extractive.

JMB (Jack Manning Bancroft, Bundjalung man and Indigenous change-maker) says that Dreaming energy is supernatural power that can only interact with natural systems that have limits, embedded negative feedback loops—otherwise you end up with mushroom clouds coming out of Einstein equations. An unnatural system running on limitless desire simply can't access that supernatural energy. At the same time, he says there is a tension—there is critical work to be done on energy in modern systems, but how can we help them develop in healthy ways when they seek only to extract knowledge from us for unhealthy purposes? How can we do this work in the knowledge economies of empires, in institutions that kill the relationships holding our knowledge?

Chels talks about the attraction between negative and positive ions, and about the measurable energies that are constantly flowing through and from us throughout our lives—potential, kinetic, metabolic, chemical, gravitational—all in reproductive closed loops. She says the attraction between these particles potentially keeps them together after we die, entering other forms as they move and change. These self-organising energies are not resources to be harvested and stored for consumption, not without killing the entities that are shaped around them.

JD rumbles in a voice like rocks about the energy systems of land containing affordances that signal relational processes for energy use, and that these are currently being destroyed on his Country by natural gas fracking. Why steal fire if you're creating a void where no fire can burn?

Josh Waters, a Gamilaroi student of complexity science, says you can't remove processes from their systems of origin and expect them to work. You can't convert hydrogen to helium for fusion energy, replicating solar functions outside of the system that is our sun. That's playing with fire. Time-place is also a variable that causes these experiments to fail again and again—we know that if you burn the grass in one time-place, this gives rise to regeneration at a later time-place. Evolutionary energy is vast, but it occurs over deep time within the limits of scale. There are co-evolutionary constraints, epigenetics as regulatory feedback loops that prevent exploitation and accumulation of this energy in any single time-place, for any single species or entity. Patterns evolve, but only in step with every other connected system. Cambrian explosions are total systems increase events, not micro-level events to elevate one system above all others.

As usual, Josh has been sitting quietly for the entire yarn then comes in at the end with some ingenious way of tying it all together. He suggests that the physical laws of our land cannot tolerate asymmetry between inputs and outputs, and this is how zero-point energy works. Temporary closed systems form and are eradicated as creation rushes in to fill the void. He says this only occurs in very small-scale systems, like the foot pads of gecko lizards. Momentary voids allow gecko toes to stick to any surface, but it's probably a good thing that this phenomenon can't scale for something as big as a crocodile.

For some reason all I can think of is serpent story from Kuranda in north Queensland. It's a new story, reporting a recent event that occurred in the last ten thousand years. The people there experimented with currency, using rare spiral shells for fungible tokens as a store of value in trading relationships. It worked for a while, until blackbird people noticed the great serpent had many of these shells stuck between his scales from his seasonal journeys beneath the sea. So they waited for him to come down the ridge, ambushed him and killed him for the shells. The resulting hoard of tokens that did not represent tangible, relational exchanges must have created an energetic void which creation rushed to fill with true value, sucking life and relatedness out of the land and people there. The cautionary tale of this heist was left behind so that all would remember the cataclysm that followed and avoid making the same economic mistake again.

What was that mistake? Well, I guess any exchange within healthy trade relationships creates temporary voids of debt that attract people together until their mutual relatedness fills the space between them with abundant energy. Scaling those voids of debt beyond the limits of local human relationships generates ravenous entities with the capacity to swallow Greece and not even burp after. Have I strayed from the topic of this yarn? Well, JMB assures me money *is* energy, so maybe not. The yarn dies out as it inevitably takes a dull turn towards funding now, as we figure out how to bring in enough money to keep the lights on in our lab.

This has calmed me a little bit, taking my mind back into the Wanjau yarns and getting that metallic snake to stop spinning inside my head. How easy life would be if all my relationships and interactions still sat within the

Law like this. And that's how I'm just like you and everybody else in the world right now—I think things would be better if everyone was just like me, and I'm mad as hell that they're not. Wanjau is not for everybody, I have to admit. It's a complex process and almost nobody has time for it. Also, it doesn't have any simple, viral memes or patterns of weaponised rhetoric to feed our outrage and entitlement, and what would we do without all that anger to power us through our days?

The whole world did a workshop recently, starting around 2016, inducting us all into the wrong story and bad relation of *The Art of the Deal*. Most of our interactions are operating from this pattern now, which means there is always a winner and a loser, and the winner is the one who tells the most lies and does the most damage. The loser says, 'Please stop that, it's hurting me,' to which the winner replies, 'I'm not doing that, you're doing that. *You're* hurting *me*. You're crazy, you're imagining things. And now you're gaslighting me! Fatty!'

The loser sputters at the outrageous physics of this 5-D chess attack, tries to deal with each lie in turn, becomes exhausted and then pathetic (and later either depressed or vindictive). Meanwhile the winner spins off into a righteous moral panic, recruiting supporters and kicking up more mendacious dust. *Stop hitting yourself. I know you are, but what am I?* For the winners in this ridiculous game, the same nastiness that worked for them in kindergarten still works today. The losers are also trapped in the patterns of helplessness they learned in their infancy.

Both roles are twisted and grounded in narcissism and entitlement, feeding into and off each other. Between every movement and every tribe, down to every tiny kinship pair, this curse is inflating wrong relation exponentially everywhere the signal can reach. (And it reaches everywhere.) The worst player wins the game, and power is the prize, in every corner of every home.

Maybe Indigenous wisdom will save the day? Not likely; The Art of the Deal is everywhere now. It's a shameful and shameless process. Flip, lie, contradict yourself, double down and yell until everything is broken, then enjoy your unearnt social advancement as you stand upon the smoking ruins of your relationships. Maggie Thatcher's curse, 'There is no such thing as society', has taken a while to reach us here because of Indigenous exclusion from the economy, but every day more of us become collateral damage in the scorched-earth policies of an economic experiment scaled to the planetary level. We can either join the horrid game and be slowly destroyed, or refuse to play and be destroyed immediately.

Every explosive phenomenon always produces a regulatory force in the end, however. Negative feedback loops inevitably emerge from chaotic systems during phase transitions, and things tend back towards stability for a while. The challenge of being a custodian is to be able to spot where potential emergence may come into being, the inflection points (that some call beginnings), and lend a little leverage for phase shifts when needed.

Brother Deen says, 'When you're walking on Country the secret is you're looking for system linkages, the open and closed loops interacting together.' He speaks from his understanding of Freshwater–Saltwater Dreaming and that liminal space in between things, where all the magic happens. That's how you know the right way to care for the land, and she'll let you know when something is wrong and in need of correction, but only if you're in right relation and capable of the right response. You need to know how to get out of your own way and let nature do the heavy lifting.

Sartre said, 'Hell is other people.' But us-two, we know it is the opposite. It's isolation that makes you a citizen of Inferno. I don't know if you have met my friend Dante Alighieri, but if you know his work you might be starting to think of me as Virgil, taking you on a tour of the circles of hell. But you'd be wrong, because the path doesn't lie on the other side of the river, but along it, and I'm not your guide—I'm just the ferryman making oar strokes and key strokes after you give me your coin.

At least our story together will not end on a mountain top via a limbic-system hijack of illusory descent followed by rapid ascent. That's just guru trickery (sorry, Brother Dante, but it is). 'Everything is terrible, but I have the answer to your suffering!' The path is not across the river, but where the river flows, and all such paths lead to the sea eventually, so my friend Pete McCurley tells me. The journey just takes a bit longer than we'd like. He smiles patiently as the river widens, because he knows us-two are going to spend the next chapter either fighting on its banks or choking on mud and slime at the bottom.

Sorry about the mess, my sibling. I wanted to demonstrate what happens when knowledge and speech are truly free, allowed to run unchecked, without the regulatory feedback loops of relational boundaries. But it got away from me like a home-made rocket. Maybe us-two need to 'clean our room', as we move through yet another circle of hell. Brace yourself for the inevitable condition that always follows the petulant entitlement of avarice: pure, unbounded rage.

Bee the Change

Originally, I made a fishing spear for this chapter, but it just made me sullen because I'd probably be arrested if I took it to the beach here, and besides, the few fish that are left in this place are too toxic to eat. So I started over and made an instrument of wrath instead—a 'bullet spear'. It's a wicked short-projectile weapon that is effective in thick scrub and confined spaces. It will fit easily in our tiny canoe and should be safe enough as long as neither of us-two has a tantrum in the next hour.

I usually keep it by the door because I've never quite shaken off the hypervigilant paranoia I developed in my youth. The spear allows me to sleep at night. It's weird I know, but hey, spears don't kill people; people kill people, and so my cold, dead hands might hold on to this vicious little tool for a bit longer, until I figure out a better way to get to sleep.

I made the bullet spear out of English privet because there's no *okanch* (native hibiscus) trees available this far south. Privet might be good for hedges in Britain, but here they seed prolifically and take over hundreds of acres in just a few seasons, choking out every bit of life in a place. For some reason people keep planting them in their gardens. Privet provides very straight, light, hard sticks, though, and like I always say, 'If life gives you privet, make spears.' I keep stories in that spear about fear, bees, disinformation, crowdsourced outrage and moral panic. It's not helping me to make sense of the world, though, because scared means stupid and the more weapons I make the more terrified I become. As you probably know, when stupid people panic, they tend to get angry and behave badly. I'm striving to avoid this outcome, without much success.

I'm on a hair-trigger as I continue looking for the one perfect thinking tool that will help me avoid the shouting matches, manipulative bullshit, rapturous escapism and cultish ideologies of this era. I can't find it, not in my culture or anyone else's. I guess my community has an aversion to one-size-fits-all solutions, so there's never one tool to rule them all, or one message, or one guru.

We go further than merely triangulating datasets to sift out the gammin (bullshit) stuff—we polyangulate within a messy and complex field, then sit with all that and yarn, then wait for patterns to emerge. Or we yell and swear and fight, then wait for patterns to emerge. Or we just wait. We're not afraid of uncertainty, so we do not need to rush to any immediate conclusions and are happy to let our stories marinate, sometimes for a few generations.

Problem is, this is way too slow when you must analyse a dozen complex situations a day just to survive this howling red-faced modernity, and there's a mountain of lies to sift through before you can find a genuine dataset or an analysis that has been conducted in good faith. Even then, as most of the analysis around any threat is conducted by old settler hacks prone to undetectable micro-strokes, even reliable analysts are likely to go off the rails and start spouting crazy shit at any moment, so you can't stick with trusted sources for too long. As a result of these chaotic non-local signals, alongside a truckload of propaganda, much of our Indigenous community has begun to stray from our traditional sense-making practices.

We're not immune to disinformation here. Every week another Elder gets radicalised by some bizarre US cult. My friend Tina Ngata, a Māori writer and activist in New Zealand, says they have the same problem over there, with an epidemic of Māori MAGA sweeping through their communities. We're just as nuts as everybody else right now, which is something you need to know in case you've come to this yarn seeking a bit of imperial nostalgia through feel-good Indigenous wisdom. You're not going to find your way through this mess in drum circles and sweat lodges, or any other weird co-opted bits and pieces of native culture that enable spiritual bypass—chanting and vison-questing and tripping balls to avoid the hard feelings that come with being authentically grounded in your shitty context. We have to look past the sexy and inspiring stuff and step up to our fear and uncertainty, before we panic and turn into a seething mosh-pit of fast zombies.

Down here in hell, the ground is littered with people who couldn't keep a leash on their misdirected wrath. They learned too late that rage is a force multiplier that should only be deployed where success is certain, collateral damage is zero and your actions will definitely make the world better for your descendants. The problem is, when we feel certain the time is right for rage, we're usually mistaken and it's our fear and narcissism taking the wheel.

Millions of T-shirts and other bits of empowering merchandise channel our passions into false certainty, telling us *Foetal Lives Matter* and *God Hates [insert minority]*. I'm getting slogan fatigue. It's harder every day to work up a bit of righteous anger over my *Always Was Always Will Be Aboriginal Land* tote bag. The merch in my house tells me *The Future Is Female*, or *The Future Is Indigenous*. Maybe it will be both, when all the old rich men retreat to their underground bunkers or blast themselves out into space. Maybe the meek will indeed inherit the earth for a while, in order to clean it up for the masters' glorious return, for a new golden age of priests and kings.

In the short term, though, the future is evaluation. Most of us are becoming irrelevant as workers and we sure as hell won't be getting our food and shelter for free, so we'll be earning our Universal Basic Incomes in digital tokens for evaluating things online. The overeducated will be peer-reviewing papers and critiquing art, while the undereducated will be rating doughnuts, TV and exper-imental medications in exchange for crypto-coupons and merch with empowering messages assuring us that what-ever demographic group we identify with will soon be great again.

So I'm sitting and cutting these ideas into the spear when an email pings up from a friend.

Once I was in Argentina and I couldn't sleep so I gazed out the window at the misty sky, thinking of how we are all united under one sky, across space and time…and then in the morning I saw that the misty sky was a concrete wall. But by that point, the wall was irrelevant. I already had the message.

The email is from Katherine Collins, a beekeeper I've been yarning with, a Celtic woman from the United States, who is the author of a book called *The Nature of Investing*, in which she explores the ways biomimicry can inform invest-ment. It's Samhain time for her, that ritual time when the

Irish hold feasts and festivals responding to a season when the spirits of the dead walk the physical world and get up to all kinds of mischief, normalising crazy thoughts and actions in public spaces. It's an auspicious moment to have our yarns about the insane fears and passions that people project onto bees.

As with all things, there is good crazy and bad crazy, then stuff that is just crazy-interesting. Katherine admits her Celtic tradition has her talking to her bees and regarding them as members of the family, which they believe keeps the bees calm and stops them from swarming. (That would be an example of good crazy, from being in good relation.) Her family is getting smaller and smaller, though. Her grandparents had a dozen children, then her parents had half that number, while her own generation of siblings has only produced two offspring.

I jokingly tell her this is part of our plan—The Great Replacement. We're going to limit the fertility of Europeans and gradually breed them out of existence (starting with that recessive redhead gene Katherine carries). That's why so many Aboriginal families have Irish names—we marry in and gradually exterminate them all by loving them to death. (That theory would be an example of bad crazy, from being in bad relation.)

'Hey Katherine!'

'Yes Tyson?'

'Did you know that Einstein said if the bees die all

life on earth would disappear within two years? And hey Katherine!'

'Yes Tyson?'

'Did you know all the bees are dying? All of them!'

This makes Katherine chuckle. That disinformation is an example of bad crazy you have to file away with 'The Great Barrier Reef will be gone in five years!' and 'All bananas will be extinct before the end of the decade!' These hot takes have been around since 2010 and they do just as much damage as climate-change denial.

I'm so tired of the lies, entitlement, outrage and bickering in this fortressed city. I have family members in jail for drinking in places where it is illegal for Aboriginal people to consume alcohol, while some idiot down at the shops yells at me for infringing her liberties because I'm wearing a face mask. 'I can't breathe,' she says. I take it off to calm her down and some other doopy prick now tells me I'm taking away his right to safety while he films me with his phone. So much noise, so little story. Still, I keep up the yarns, so I can write another book for settlers to fight about. Like there aren't enough of these books already.

You and me and Katherine can see the fallen angels guarding the exits of this city, and the furies atop its walls screaming at us about free markets, free speech and strong borders. They are calling in some powerful entity to be the agent of their retribution, and I'm too angry now to fear its arrival.

My sister was murdered recently. I can't share the details for legal and cultural reasons, so that's all I'll say about that, beyond flagging it as an explanation of the barely restrained wrath that bubbles like boiling mud throughout my yarns with Katherine. Besides, I have deadlines and too many dependents who won't be able to eat or be sheltered if I stop working, so I continue to research and write, instead of attending to this grief that will turn me to stone in the end, if I don't leave this place and deal with it soon.

So I work and wait for the police investigation to end and the funeral to begin, which will be the last of my leave used up for the year, for grief. No margaritas on a beach for me. My holidays are always death wails and shovels and dirt. Year by year, I keep the grief and fatigue at bay by swallowing blobs of rage like amphetamines.

I look forward to walking Country again without carrying a box. One day. Realistically, I probably won't return to the land until I'm in a box myself, and in that way I'm the same as you. I bet you long for some place, even if you've never seen it. I miss my place. But at least I can earn a good living by talking to an Irish woman on the other side of the planet about it, and in that way I'm more fortunate than most of the people in the world. I'm told daily that I should practise gratitude, but I do struggle with the idea of thanking an invisible man in the sky for giving billions of people lives that are even shittier than mine, in order for some narcissist to buy himself a bigger boat.

I tell Katherine our land is sugarbag country, which means it's flowing with honey but not a lot of milk. We have stingless social bees that are smaller than flies, so we don't have to worry about being stung when we harvest the honey. These tiny miracles exist in a sub-equatorial belt around the world, so you can find them in South America, South Africa and a bunch of Pacific islands. The *wom* (wax) in these hives is black, and the central brood where the babies are housed has a unique spiral shape, formed from the same patterning of hexagonal nodes created by every bee species on the planet. There are volumes of sacred geometry to be found here, but Katherine and I find more breathless wonder in the potential utility of more mundane bee maths.

Katherine says the hexagon is the most efficient structure in creation, a mathematical solution utilising the least possible amount of material for the largest and strongest shape that you can make. In terms of efficiency, multiple hexagonal containers can store a substance in a small space better than any other arrangement. We think this could be a great packaging solution that could solve a lot of problems if combined with seaweed packaging technology from Scandinavia. But Katherine laments that the miracle of the hexagon is most widely used in the design of corporate logos.

The hexagon pattern is fairly uniform in domestic hives, but I tell Katherine that in native hives it is only used in the brood—the rest of the hive is a chaotic bubbling mass that looks like something from the *Alien* movies. But there's still pattern in that chaos to be discerned, the same way you can see governance and communication patterns in the anarchy of a swarm. I see story there, but I can also see energy-efficient coding, dark data processing, extended cognition driving autopoietic computation and distributed decision-making. There is always a signal from the earth to be found in the patterns of chaos.

I used to keep native beehives, but they can't survive this far south—it's too bloody cold. Megan keeps domestic bees in our small suburban backyard here, and I don't know much about them, so I assist her as we wade through swarms in our big white spacesuits. These European bees are high maintenance. It's strange that the tamer a creature becomes, the more aggressively needy it gets. It's particularly hard in this season, when more queens are hatched and the hive forms angry factions and groups of defectors. There are coups and assassinations and civil wars. We call it the Game of Thrones season.

'Hey Katherine!'

'Yes Tyson?'

'Sometimes they breed with African varieties and become Africanised bees! They're aggressive and angry and they kill people! They even kill children and pets!'

Katherine laughs about the moral panics that have flared up periodically in her country around the pseudo-science of 'Africanised' bees, usually in step with cycles of indignation and punitive policy directed towards human 'super preda-tors' in certain 'urban communities'.

She is frustrated about the manufactured noise that has been inserted into the interface between modern humans and nature. 'We're supposed to be part of it, but the stories we lay over the top of this relationship often become twisted, particularly with bees. The same goes with finance.'

I agree with her. Sugarbag stories are supposed to have a unifying effect, weaving things together under sacred entities of rainbow, moon, hollow trees and the hollows beneath the earth. Hero ancestors follow the bees in our creation stories and landscapes are formed in the process. But Shakespeare talks of bees in terms of kings and armies of flying soldiers.

Katherine says similar militarised narratives and meta-phors also taint the natural sciences and asserts again that this is echoed in the discipline of finance. 'If it's not military metaphors, it's sports, which is the same thing but slightly adapted. I try to replace military terms with natural concepts to change the conversation, like "emerge" and "evolve", so that people can see finance as more of a system and less of a machine.'

'Hey Katherine!'

'Yes Tyson?'

'The Bible says, "And the Amorites, which dwelt in that mountain, came out against you, and chased you, as bees do, and destroyed you." And Katherine?'

'What else does it say, Tyson?'

'"They compass me about like bees; they are quenched as the fire of thorns; for in the name of the Lord I will destroy them!"'

This makes me think I'd prefer to have someone tell me, 'I'm from the government and I'm here to help,' rather than, 'I'm from the government and I'm here to punish the enemies of God!'

Katherine tells me that the biblical stories of bees often use militarised language, while the resources of the hive signify peace and abundance—lands of milk and honey. She notes that New Age narratives are projected the same way onto the bee—as a spirit animal that manifests abundance. She prefers this, however, to the opposite narratives of killer bees. She thinks both ends of the political spectrum have very little accuracy or utility when it comes to bees or money or anything else.

This makes me think I'd prefer to have someone tell me, 'I'm from the government and I'm here to punish the enemies of God,' rather than, 'I'm from the government and I'm here to balance your chakras.'

'It all falls into its proper proportions if you're connected to a place or creature; you can see all the layers in between these two extremes in context, because you know what's in between. But there are so many settings now where we don't have that context. We don't have that connection, so we only have these two poles to orient ourselves and neither one is satisfying or even accurate in isolation. Reconnecting is at the root of so many things. It's tempting to want to skip over that and just take your bee spirit-animal card and go forward. Because whoa, it's some serious work—it's the work of a lifetime.'

She cautions against centrism too, however, asserting that the political spectrum is really more like a saucer than a continuum—the edges of it are real, but they have no depth and hold no water. While there's bliss to be found at the high ground around the edges, there is little joy, which can only be found in the deeper places. Those places aren't easy, though, and you get stung from time to time.

We share our bee-sting stories. Mine is about the time I bought a hive for Megan's birthday, secretly stashing it out the back as a surprise, while I got stung over thirty times on my belly trying to manhandle it into position. I had to hide the pain to keep the gift a surprise, but she could see something was wrong that I wasn't telling her, which made her upset, and we had a big fight.

'Look, there's your bees, happy fuckin' birthday!'

'I don't want 'em. Fuck you.'

'Nah, fuck you.'

'Nah, fuck *you*.'

Katherine laughs but then tactfully tells me, 'I've never been stung where I didn't deserve it.'

Katherine's sting stories are mostly swarming disasters during that frantic Game of Thrones season when new queens emerge. We agree that this is the time when you find out about your neighbours—there's nothing that brings out the rage in people more than a bee swarm.

Over the deafening hum we often hear loud complaints from nearby residents, as people call the local council to complain about 'The Aborigines next door!'

'It's one rule for them and one rule for us!'

And (I assume they're talking about the bees), 'You have to send someone around to remove them.'

And weirdly, 'While you're at it, somebody has to do something about these cooking shows telling me to eat native foods! It's a slippery slope!'

Suddenly there's old-school bigotry on display that we haven't seen since before we moved to this 'nice' street, and like any good shit-stirrer I escalate the tension by hanging the Aboriginal flag out front and making bets with my friends about how long it will take before somebody tries to tear it down and I have to get my spear out. But there's nothing like that in this neighbourhood, just an increase in how many banana cakes are exchanged with everyone but us, and gossipy chats with plenty of headshaking over cups of tea, up and down the street.

I realise there is a positive outcome here—we've helped our neighbours strengthen and renew their community relationships with each other. I'm happy enough about my role in creating that little glimmer of pre-nineties social cohesion. There were a couple of visits and inspections from local officials after that, but I'm a respectable savage now, so there were none of the police raids and abductions I've experienced in the past.

Katherine winces and says there's something about bees that brings out both the best and worst in people. I'm just grateful she is engaging and staying in good relation with me, instead of retreating into some yarn-terminating cliché like 'I'm just here to shut my privileged mouth and listen' or trying to be my ally or apologising or chanting slogans and acknowledgments. We have right story together, bee story, and she's honouring that connection by riffing on my narratives of complaint to find wider contexts and meaning.

She says it's like making sense of the complexities of the pandemic—it's hard to tell what's being caused and what's being revealed. As the board chair of the Santa Fe Institute, which is a leading institution in the science of complexity, she is interested in distinguishing between causation and correlation, but also preconditions that might be revealed by a crisis and mistaken as a result of that crisis. There is a difference between true emergence and just noticing something for the first time.

She talks about a recent firefly study out of the institute in which they tried replicating results from other studies but changed standpoints between viewing at a distance and viewing from among the dance of those insects. They found novel patterns that were not emergent, but had been there all along. Story and standpoint matter, and you need many of them to understand how a system works.

Attachment to a singular narrative is like pinning an insect to a board and measuring it: if you aren't watching it in flight, you're missing the point.

Narrative underpins all good sense-making, but also all the most terrible conflicts. Katherine asks, 'What is a good outcome with the hive? Maximising honey production or exposing them to the least amount of pesticides?' She says the beekeeping community fights on social media over such competing narratives. 'In real life it's a great community but online it's war! Factions, big time—vicious.'

'Hey Katherine.'

'What Tyson?'

'Did you know that according to the laws of physics, bees shouldn't be able to fly, but somehow they do? Did you know that?'

Katherine guffaws and enjoys this good bit of what the Irish call *craic*. But still, it's not enough to tempt her into condemnation of silly thinking.

'The capacity for wonder is such a gift but sometimes we wonder in a way that is a little misguided. But you know, when you have that true sense of wonder, it's such a powerful and sophisticated signal and we're taught to dismiss it so quickly. So I've been trying to retrain myself to just stop before I turn it into something intellectual or frivolous. Just sit still for a minute. It's a capacity we haven't nurtured for a while. Try not to project too much and just allow space for wonder.'

'Do you know what else Katherine?'

'What?'

'In the Quran, written fourteen hundred years ago, it says the male bees stay in the hive and the females go out for honey, and that there is a queen.'

'That long ago?'

'They knew that before western science, which only figured it out recently!'

My stage-whispered provocations are only making her laugh, so I change gears and ask her about her disastrous CNBC interview. In that yarn she was asked about where she stood on growth versus degrowth. She responded that weight gain from a pregnancy is a wonderful thing, but it's not so great if it comes from eating too much pizza. This upset people from every point on the political spectrum, so her inbox was filled with hate mail for a month.

'Profit—you can get there by pillaging or you can get there by creating, and there is nothing on a spreadsheet to tell you which it is. Degrowth needs a new brand. My question is: growth of what? You can easily have an economy growing in a less stuff-intensive way, but increasing in value in terms of health, joy, et cetera; or you can have an economy that is growing while everything is being destroyed. So the growth versus degrowth debate is grounded in the wrong question.'

I share my thoughts on price and value, the way things are priced according to limitability and excludability, the way supply and demand equilibrium is sold to us as proof that free markets solve every problem—if you cut down most of the trees, then they become scarce and therefore expensive, so fewer people can afford wood and the trees grow back! I ask if this mythical equilibrium is actually possible, or just some oligarch's fantasy.

'It's not quite a lie but it sure isn't a truth. It's a really simple way to model a moment in time. The trouble is, we don't live in the model, and we don't live in a moment in time. We live ongoing. This is the root that is poorly placed of neoclassical economics and therefore most finance. The math is zero-sum math. The first thing you learn in Economics 101 is this phrase *ceteris paribus*, which means "all else being equal", and you put the letters CP in the corner to show that you're recognising that everything you just proved is "all things being equal". That's a lie. All else is never equal in this connected world.'

I quip that this is the economic equivalent of disclaimers like, 'I'm not racist but…' or 'Some of my best friends are…'

'The math is accurate and sometimes helpful, but the limitations are severe, and we set all those limitations in the corner. For way too long, in a kind of shameful way, we knew better and we still did it for a hundred years. Because of that, the math of neoclassical economics is based on a zero-sum fixed pie and there are two fatal flaws to that. One is that it sets you up for this magical equilibrium theorem that never actually happens in real life, and it teaches you that everything is either/or, win/lose, yes/no. Bullshit. If you're really a great investor it's the creation process that has the value—you're going to foster something of value in the world that didn't exist before. You haven't just pillaged. But the idea in the investment market is that if you're doing something beneficial for the environment, by definition you are guaranteed to make less money no matter what. Says who? There is almost zero evidence for that, but it's a deep root.'

She muses that this limited framing is just like the forced choice of believing the bee is either a spirit guide or an Africanised monster coming to kill your children. 'It's way messier and harder to try to model the world as it really is, but my gosh how much more interesting.'

Nothing is entirely true or entirely false. That's why we have theories—you're supposed to be able to move from one story to the next depending on the context, for a place, for a season—Newton when you're playing pool, Einstein when you're using your phone and you want the satellite signal to work. Neither of those theories is completely true, but one wins you money when you're gambling at the pub and the other wins you money when you're gambling online.

'When learning new things, we are trained to think *Is this true or false?* But it is so much better to think *When will this be useful?* Also, *When should I not rely on this? When will it fall apart?'*

'Hey Katherine!'

'Yes Tyson?'

'Did you know there are zombie bees who leave the hive at night and fly around?'

'Ha ha ha ha!'

'Yeah, it's the flight of the living dead.'

When Katherine studied biology under Janine Benyus, who coined the term 'biomimicry', she took comfort in generalisable design principles of nature, such as systems running on sunlight, being both efficient and effective, and using recyclable materials.

'This is how the world functions. Oh my goodness! The growth versus degrowth argument has become polarised and misses what is interesting that can be learned from life. In education you are rewarded for having an opinion and defending it while defeating opposing opinions. You're not rewarded for saying, *well it depends,* or *maybe,* even though that's way more accurate and productive. When I find myself digging in my heels, as a practice now I try to give the most persuasive opposite argument—I want to not be too settled.'

But who wants to invest in that kind of nuance? Accounting measures *things,* not actions and relationships. Capital demands predictability, uniformity, stability—but also crises to leverage, and sublime miracles to vindicate faith in the invisible hand of the marketplace. Maybe that's why economists keep trying to freeze moments of supply–demand equilibrium in time. The powerful have a conflicted longing for both liminal moments of epiphany and stable truths. Both are profitable, in terms of litres of honey sold and millions of clicks on the monetised zombie bees article, while signals of change in public sentiment and global climate are drowned in all the noise, and business continues as usual.

'Once a new idea starts to get accepted, the response is to splosh it into the machine of all the old ideas. It's like diversity policies. *Oh, come into our company and I'll train you to be just like all the other people in our company!* I see the same thing with ideas in sustainability. *Oh, I'll condense this down into a number and put it into this model and then my portfolio optimiser tool doesn't really have to change at all.* I don't think that's going to get us there.'

'Hey, Tyson!'

'Yes, Katherine?'

'Did you know the queen bee is forced to mate all day long and is never allowed to leave the hive?'

'Wow, Katherine. No, I didn't know that. I'll remember that next time I'm chasing one of them down the street in my spacesuit.'

Damn Katherine. That's some good *craic*. The Irish I've met all seem to know that every yarn needs a bit of messy play and laughter.

'Ultimately the messy conversation is going to win because it's closer to the actual world. The ice palace only works until it gets too hot. In the end it comes down to fear. People become comfortable with stability and fear the messiness of complexity.'

Katherine's greatest hope for the historical phase shift we are living through is the next generation of thinkers who are bringing contextual awareness and wonder to the table.

'My younger colleagues are living in a non-dualistic world. If your opening premise is not either/or, then all things are possible.'

Although it's customary to sneer at the idealism of youth, like Katherine I'm finding myself impressed with the next generation. Sure, they have performative ways of dealing with trauma that are unfamiliar to me, as though demographically categorised ordeals can be transformed into some kind of social capital and then speculated on in an ideological futures market. But their way can't be any worse than mine, which usually involves privately ripping my spirit to shreds and scattering it across the earth while I dig all the graves for my loved ones and cut down all the trees for my masters. My fellow traveller Pete McCurley seems to think there's another way through trauma, but I don't know what it is. I hope he tells me one day.

The wi-fi has dropped out, so Katherine can't help us find the answer either.

What I do know is that trauma doesn't come from the abuses we suffer—it comes from our loss of dignity afterwards and the failure to make sense of it all by processing it together with our relations. We feel guilt, which is a bit like shame but removed from the collective—individualised, bespoke and driven inwards. It's not the violence of my youth that keeps me up at night; it's the shame of that terrible noise I made when I eventually broke down and begged, 'No, no, please stop.' I fell into the habit of payback after that. Denial of reality and right relation is why I fear, why I rage and why I keep my spear by the door.

In my failure to make sense of trauma, I have convinced myself that I have a right to safety and dignity, but am confronted daily with the fact that this is an illusion. So I weave introspective narratives of outrage and they keep me warm, while I try to keep that monster, that pathetic, weeping ghost-of-Tyson-past at bay. No more. The other day I found myself making that same disgusting begging noise for the first time in decades, *please stop, please stop,* a sound I haven't made since the day I grew strong enough to smash my tormentor's nose and blacken its eyes. But my spear was suddenly of no use to me, because I was pleading with someone I love. Our enemies are seldom strangers outside our gates.

I've been hoping to catch a glimpse of my old tormentor down here in hell, getting ripped to shreds by its peers. I imagined myself standing in our canoe and shoving that bastard's head beneath the putrid water with my booted foot. But us-two need to move on now before this place gets its teeth into us. Pete reckons there's a place of balance that's not a temporary equilibrium, and I think I can see what he's talking about.

In the end it's not about the sting or the honey. It's about...

Oh shit, here comes the grief. Rivers of it.

I have to fly home now, to help carry a box.

How about you finish that thought for us? This is supposed to be a yarn, after all.

The Riddle of Steel

I try to avoid setting up comparisons with other cultures that suggest my people are superior beings (a practice that seldom ends well, historically), but if I may, I would like to suggest that we do death better than most people.

We run two funerals these days—one adapted from traditional practice, and then a church funeral the day after that. The church funeral doesn't help much and can end with people fighting around an open grave, but the traditional one carries indescribable healing magics that we create collectively. It is a highly structured sequence of processions, wailing, singing, dancing and more, and the ceremonies and stages of grieving continue for a year afterwards. There is no other therapy like it on the planet that I've seen, and it makes you into an extremely high-functioning mourner. The ceremonies I've been doing over the last week back up home have really turned my tides.

I share this with you to let you know I'm okay. It's not my place or the role of this book to 'capture' this cultural process for you; we're not doing anthropology (where you report on my life to others), or auto-ethnography (where I report on my life to you). Remember, we're partners in this heretical act of looking out at the world together through a glitchy Indigenous lens and riffing on what we see there. We're inquiring *through* Indigenous knowledge, not *about* it, and this is a deeply unsettling and unpopular process in a world that gobbles up minority narratives and wisdom like chocolate-covered strawberries and macadamias. So we're paddling our canoe into a new circle of hell, with all our friends who have been banished as heretics for looking beyond the nuts and berries, the paint and feathers and palaeo woo-woo.

When we have our gaze set on an idealised past or a mythical future, we miss our chance to engage with right story in the present. Cultural longevity is important, but living cultures must always adapt to current contexts and remain fluid enough to allow for continual emergence. No entity is immortal. With that in mind, I have a story for you that is modern, urban and far from exotic, to explain how

I first got interested in Dante, who is the reason us-two are taking our canoe on this tour of hell.

It was sometime in my late teens, I'm not sure when, but I was struggling through Dante's *Commedia* while trying to figure out how to navigate life in a town. I was reading books daily because I couldn't afford a TV. I preferred Stephen King at the time, but the classics were way cheaper, and I was always broke. I chose Dante because I thought I was in love with an Italian girl who was way out of my league, and I wanted to impress her. She was a Calabrian princess and I was an itinerant savage, a swarthy criminal with a drinking problem and a dead cockroach stuck inside his ear, so it was a long shot at best. I spent the best part of a year studying Dante's language and work, while admiring the *principessa* from afar and working hard for her entrepreneur father for seven bucks an hour. Kitchen prep. Making coffee. Beating people up.

One day I worked up the courage to approach the princess and slip *The Divine Comedy* casually into conversation to make it seem like I had hidden depths of sophisticated knowledge—like there was more to me than met the eye. I tried to recite passages I had memorised in her language, but she rolled her eyes and said, 'Aw my gaaawd, you're such an idiot!' and slipped her tongue into my mouth. She then whispered in my ear that she'd been in love with me since the day she saw me beat up a fella who came looking for her dad with a meat cleaver. It was paradise for about five minutes, finding each other there, until her brother shouted at her and called her a slut. She ran off and I never saw her again after that. Thanks a million, Guido.

It turns out that horrible stupid little words and deeds are way more powerful than a master work of western literature. It really is easier to break shit than to make shit, in this global culture of reason and progress. Still, I sat on *The Divine Comedy* like an egg for over three decades, and when it hatched for me, this book came out. Find what hope you may in this story, although when you dance with Dante, the fine print says you have to abandon that sacred cow before you enter.

For these heretical yarns, I've set aside my wood-carving tools and taken up the hammer and anvil, as I contemplate all this entropy on the Tree of Woe, surrounded by a multitude of iconoclasts in shallow graves. Nearby, there is a tomb with an ancient sword inside, waiting for us to discover it and marvel at the affordances of power it offers. Ghostly voices whisper warnings in this desolate graveyard. *There is a price, barbarian!* Power always comes at a cost that is more than we can bear. Hot steel is our medium for the yarns in this chapter, as us-two move deeper into hell, hoping that this will all end with an emergence into paradise.

At the forge, it occurs to me that I used to make tools for music, communication and hunting, but for the last couple of years all the carvings I've created have been weapons of war. I strike the stinking, white-hot metal at Pete McCurley's smithy, trying to make a little steel barramundi sculpture, but halfway through it turns into a punch-dagger, alerting me to the fact that I might have a problem. What kind of wrong story am I carrying if everything I make turns out this way?

All my writing comes from my carving, so I can only conclude that I've begun to weaponise my words as well, and I don't want to be an information warrior. I've given myself one boomerang, a spear tip and a few pages of yarns to try and figure out how to reverse this cultural sacrilege and end my contrarian assault on the world. I need to figure out how to heal my relationships with the occupying powers and systems I hate so much; find a way to live beside them for a bit, while they finish off the last of the living goddamn planet. Bloody hell, this is going to be hard.

So I'm back at Pete's place working with him at the forge. There is a blackwood fallen across the fence out front. It might have blocked the gate, but the lightning bolt that dropped it made it fall the other way, so I think maybe the land and the old people might not disapprove of me being here, since they could easily have blocked the gate with that tree and stopped me from driving in. Too quickly, I take this as tacit ancestral approval of my experimentation with unsustainable materials, as long as I follow the traditional processes and protocols for makers in our culture.

Part of that process is maintaining an awareness of signs in the landscape, communications from sentient systems of land and ancestors. There is some superstition in my science, but that's the part that demands rigour and adherence to ethical protocols. What else could provide the motivation to attend to these things? Material reality produces individual incentives for deception and destruction; spirit provides ancestral incentives for truth and care. We need spirit, whether it exists or not, if we want to thrive as people-in-place. So I think again about the lightning. The blackwood tree fell the other way, but still it fell. I should stop to take in that message, because there are devils about, although I am almost too excited about blacksmithing to notice. I swing the hammer rhythmically, entranced, and flash back into long-forgotten patterns of thought and behaviour.

I'm a kid, running and lifting stones and logs to make myself strong like Conan the Barbarian. I'm humming the soundtrack of that movie as I drive my limbs forward, punching fence posts and head-butting rusty barrels of Agent Orange stashed in the bush by belligerent pastoralists. I throw old axes and cane knives at ironbark trees until I'm a force to be reckoned with. Aaaarghiyaaaahiyaaah! I bellow at the world. I misquote Nietzsche, like the caption did at the start of the film, so I'm certain that what doesn't kill me will only make me stronger. I quote Khan more accurately, as Schwarzenegger himself does, and 'drive my enemies before me and hear the lamentations of their women'. In quiet moments I contemplate the Riddle of Steel (a thought experiment I can't understand, as big Arnie never quite explained it properly), because that's about as tender as a boy is allowed to get on the frontier of this empire if he wants to survive the Wheel of Pain.

The romance of the forge wears off quickly. What were they thinking when they invented this technology? It's horrible! The EROI (energy return on investment) is almost non-existent at the local scale, and I can see why the entire process from ore to product requires ruinous exploitation of land and people in order to scale up for any kind of payoff. My arms are killing me from swinging the hammer all day and burning a truckload of fossil fuel to melt a bit of damaged rock and hasten the heat death of the universe. It's ridiculous.

Between the excitement, romance and back pain, I forget to pay proper respects to the steel and its story. I want to replicate the results of one of Pete's previous experiments, when he made a steel boomerang from a piece of antique timber-mill equipment. The steel had revealed its memory of all the trees it had cut through in the old days, with a wood-grain pattern ghosted across its surface as the boomerang was completed. I want to reproduce the same process with a piece of steel from the bottom of the ocean— my hypothesis is that this boomerang will reveal the patterns of the sea. But my method is rubbish because I leap into the experiment like a barbarian and ignore the protocols that are essential to Indigenous methodologies.

We are trying to make a steel boomerang out of the keel

pin from a nineteenth-century sailing ship that was wrecked off the coast of New South Wales while carrying luxury goods to the proto-oligarchs of a new colony. We have the notion that something historically ugly can be reforged into something beautiful, and that the steel might give us some kind of message about hope and forgiveness to share with the world. We rush into this process without asking the steel its story, so all we learn in the end is that you can't polish a turd. Or, to put it a nicer way, you can't build sustainable systems on top of destructive processes.

We forget that rocks have memory, and steel is made from rocks. In our metaphysics, information is absorbed into minerals and stays there. This is why stones can contain 'bad spirit' that you don't want to mess with. You can melt them down and repurpose them, but the story remains, whether good or bad.

Well, this artefact of invasion is no different, and even white-hot it stinks of blood and piss and salt. The glowing steel cracks and falls apart, except for one piece that we retrieve and shape into a spear tip, which we fix to the end of a long shaft before quitting for the day to sleep on it and wait for some more brothers to arrive.

Another day now, and you, me and Pete are disturbed to find that the bright steel of the spear tip has cracked through the middle overnight. After we mutter about that for a while, we sit and yarn with two fellas who are traditional wood carvers also seeking some answers to the Riddle of Steel. They aren't conflicted, and don't regard the forge as a heresy, because they are clear on their purpose and continuity with land, ancestors and community. They're here to forge tools specifically for making their dish-like woomeras (spear throwers), and they spend time with the scrap metal, salvaged from old pioneer tools, to come into relation with it before smashing away at it with a big hammer. As usual, we spend a lot of hours yarning first, before we get to work.

We share our trouble with the keel-bolt steel, and eventually agree that the ocean hasn't finished its work with it yet, so we need to take it back to that place on the coast. We have to take a road trip and throw that spear far out into the sea, so the fellas give Pete one of their beautiful woomeras to keep and lend some power to the throw on that day. That's how we will undo the disrespectful process of how we made it. We had been eager to spark some kind of reconciliation magic by turning invasion-fleet artefacts into boomerangs, but healing isn't a thing to be rushed, not if you want it to last.

'So, full agreed. That spear tip was dicking around. Playing silly buggers, is what my family says.'

Pete speaks and we listen because he knows his minerals, and this time the woomera-making tools come into being in our minds before the forge is even lit.

'With steel you've got to be methodical. Precise. You've gotta know who you're working with and where it's been. In that way it's a good process. You've gotta pay close attention the whole way or you've got nothing. There's a heap of specific knowledge that pertains to its transformation points. Carbon percentage. The big one is the quench, for carbon tool steels.

'That's the temperature where it does its magic trans-formation act from soft ductile to hard brittle state. That temperature varies. You can work backwards to figure that out. Slow down. Test your questions. The way it sparks when grinding is one of the languages. Some sparks pop and dance about. That keel bolt we were annoying sparked dull red and sluggish. Its previous heat cycles have some bearing too. History matters. But you can find that right temperature threshold with a magnet—it will stop sticking when the temperature is right.

'Next step is to rapidly drop the temperature. That's where you dip it in oil or water. After that full hard quench, the steel is brittle. Glassy. Like a knapped stone tool without the benefits. That's where the temper cycles come in, to decrease hardness and increase toughness. That's done with cycles of lower heat and resting periods.

'You lost your temper, bro.'

Dearest Australia, I'm sorry for charging off half-cocked and angry, failing to come into right relation with a piece of your cultural heritage before messing around with it and ultimately ruining it. Then I blamed it (and you) for its ruin, which is unforgivable. My eyes were focused so much on the future that I lost sight of the past, and the problematic present became completely invisible to me. Does it count that I had good intentions when I did it? Probably not, no. Sorry.

I can't help myself. I'm still too disrespectful to learn the secrets of steel. I know the old fellas have a song cycle for that up north in the Gulf country, and I did once meet a fella there whose totems were anchor, machete and stingray, but that was a long time ago. I haven't met anyone whose totem is a computer yet, and I'm wondering if the elders are waiting for Moore's Law to implode and slow its insanely fast cycles of innovation and obsolescence, so they can include a motherboard in the totemic system that might last as long as a machete does. At the moment, mechanical totems would need to be abandoned and upgraded every two years, which is a timeframe that doesn't really work in our knowledge systems.

I'm reluctant to call a ceasefire in my war on digital imperialism and wait for everyone to discover an ethical innovation process. History makes it fairly clear that you should never cease hostilities until there is a treaty on the table. Not that my petty critiques make a speck of difference in the world. Indigenous tech experts are few and far between, but they're out there, and most of them aren't happy with me throwing spears at the Google bus. Many are cheerleaders for progress and transhumanism, claiming to be Indigenising the industry, but this usually just means, 'I'm Indigenous and this is tech, so I'm doing Indigenous tech.'

I keep telling them, 'You can't just paint some dots on a Fitbit and call it a digital walkabout. You can't make an Indigenous chatbot by uploading some anthropological data-sets for content—you have to get right in there and change the decision trees in that bot, change the structures of reason and protocol and teach it Aboriginal logic. Then you might have something you can call Indigenous tech.' But I think this is a fool's errand too. Why should we help mad, dying empires tinker with technologies that can only last until the rare-earth metals are all gone, and the planet is covered in radioactive waste from its processing? My colleagues don't like this at all, so they get wild at me and I go home crying to Megan, 'Waaaah! The other Indigenous thinkers won't play with me!' And she gives me a biscuit and a *kapati* and tells me it's my own damn fault.

After my failure at the forge, I decide maybe I haven't been patient or respectful enough to understand these rocks, these rare earth metals and silicon sands that are far more subtle than steel. So I decide to set aside my prejudice and learn how to code.

I start respectfully, with the same protocol you apply coming into any new land—learning the language. I choose Python as an easy code to begin with and am soon integrating systems and playing around with PyTorch to understand some basic automation. Before long I develop a database of species parameters in a familiar river system, including breeding, migration and peak fat cycles. When I am happy with it, I test it by adding an invasive carp species, running through a dozen iterations until the *nyiingk kuchan* (freshwater sharks) wipe them all out over a couple of wet seasons.

Then I learn how to do a three-layer neural net using JavaScript and from there factor in seasonal increase ceremonies, creating a prototype of an AI that will alert Elders to changes in climate and biodiversity trends requiring adjustment of ritual song cycles and land management activities annually. Now I'm figuring out how to incorporate nano-tech sensors and IoT (the Internet of Things) so that this system can be responsive to minute changes to the river system in real time. Elders will receive daily notifications, with the end goal of making caring for the land a fully automated process, in which Aunty gets some crypto every time a smart contract is created online for permission to do some strip-mining.

Only kidding. Jesus, I haven't done any of that! Of course I haven't! I'm way too lazy. Also, Megan would kill me if I did, because blockchain is her PhD topic so I'm not allowed to do anything digital unless it's with her, because she owns the rights to the entire field of IT in our house. I still get to talk to a lot of technologists, though, because mostly they don't want to yarn about their technical work, but rather seek assistance in designing the ideal world they want to build in the image of their favourite demon. They always want to do weird thought experiments with me that seem to be grooming me for a secret society of eugenicists. These generally involve psychotic scenarios with runaway trams or sinking ships and you have seconds to choose who gets to live and who gets to die. 'I know, it's terrible, but if you *had* to choose…'

In the end, I think the message from the rare-earth and silicon machines is the same as from the steel in the forge. People, like all entities, leave traces of their story in the minerals they touch. When the minerals are formed into tools, they become part of a kind of extended cognition, another part of our minds and bodies. There is a kind of cyborg relation here, but it's not a one-way street—the tool is not just an extension of your will, because you are also influenced by the design of the tool and the spirit of the minerals within it.

It's been troubling me lately that I feel like I'm not really using voice recordings and headphones and transcripts and a laptop to write this book, but that increasingly those things are writing a book and I'm just having some datasets extracted from me by an intelligence that is not my own. These tools certainly have been moving my hand a lot more than my culture has been, and I know they have a kind of sentience. I also know I'm in bad relation with them and this means my tools keep glitching out on me. Hell, I am glitching out too.

My good friend Danie Mellor has some ideas about this. He's an Indigenous artist from the jungle around Cairns in far north Queensland, who paints rainforest scenes from infrared photography, applying a carpet-snake lens to a world where every branch has a spirit hiding behind it or within. Brother Danie started working with steel around the same time as me, etching his snake-eye jungle and the historical photos of his ancestors into metal plate. In his work, the ancestors are usually small figures that are half-hidden in the forest, but in the steel pieces they loom large, like giants, filling the frame.

I ask him for the answer to the Riddle of Steel, but he has already moved on to silicon and crystal in his thinking. He says silicon is the mineral that moves and transforms information faster than anything else, but also in fleeting ways that cannot endure. He thinks crystal is the next big thing, combining the speed of sand with the stability of stone, and shows me an article about some quartz monstrosity that Google has created to overcome the second law of thermodynamics. I give him a skin scraper made from skystone (volcanic glass) and ask him what he makes of that clever obsidian. He hasn't gotten back to me on that yet.

But I'm still a little boy fighting to be as strong as Conan the Barbarian and attempting to solve the Riddle of Steel, so I don't have time for all this hi-tech ephemera. I just need to know how the steel boomerang that Pete gave me works, because I can't find the story in there and that dissonance is itching me like blackwood sap.

Steel has memory of what has been done to it. If it has

been forged badly in the past, then it will not be reforged without weakness in the finished blade (or spear tip). Us-two tried to reforge a bad past in the same way with that old pirate keel bolt, learning only that history is like steel—you can't melt it down and beat the blood out of it on an anvil. There are ghosts in the steel, and they are fluid and tenacious and will not rest until rust claims them beneath earth, waves and sky.

Maybe everything can oxidise and corrode like steel under the right circumstances, and maybe that's the secret to disposing of toxic waste with a half-life of millennia, and the toxic histories that brood like vengeful shades among all the planet-killing chemical reserves of industry. My lab was approached for a consult recently by a start-up company whose executives said they had solved the problem of Ernest Gale's hypothesis of microbial infallibility and are ready to go to market with a product that could save the world. The hypothesis is that *somewhere or other some organism exists that can, under suitable conditions, oxidise any substance which is theoretically capable of being oxidised.*

Essentially, these people have figured out how to break down almost any material in a short time into a benign goo. They wanted us to run some thought experiments using Indigenous knowledge to identify any issues that might arise if the product went to market, and we concluded that this innovation could either save the world or completely destroy it, depending on whether it was accompanied by an equally advanced, planetary-scale social technology that could ensure for all time that the goo-maker could never be weaponised. We never heard back from them.

Since the first sword emerged from the first forge, humans have been struggling to find the right social technology to balance the needs of flesh, land and overpowered tech. The only thing that can meet this challenge is right story, which must never be authored by individuals, but crowdsourced over time by people in communicative relation with the land. This is the uniquely human process that has always been facilitated by riddles, yarns and thought experiments. The Riddle of Steel in the film *Conan the Barbarian* is a good example of this process, a quest to find right story as a regulatory social technology for a tool that has been scaled outside of right relation and deployed for widespread destruction.

My great friend Arlo Davis, a native Alaskan brother who is as comfortable firing his AR-15 rifle as he is hunting with a seal spear, was also enthralled by Conan as a child. He has no problem using steel or even plastic in his tool-making. For example, he showed me a massive spear he made out of synthetic materials for hunting a large, dangerous creature with white fur. He doesn't see the use of synthetic materials in making this spear as some kind of native heresy, because he is still working from the protocols of right story. For example, he and I can never say the name of the animal the spear is intended for when talking about the weapon, because the animal will hear his name called and know that Arlo is coming for him (and that would end badly). Arlo has also worked at solving Conan's Riddle of Steel, grounded in his grandfather's protocols of blade carrying, storage and use.

'What the knife blade represents is our conscience, our sense of right and wrong. When something arises in our conscience—the decision to do something or not do something—before that moment in time and after that moment in time, there's the moment itself, which is the cutting edge of that knife. We have to deal with making the decision at the cutting edge. And in that moment, you and I and everyone in the world are the same. I haven't figured out deeply enough what the hell I'm talking about, because if that's true then ugh—what the hell does that mean about me and Hitler? Ugh! Either I haven't gone deep enough or I'm just talking out of my ass.'

Arlo and I both agree that Conan never arrives at a true answer to the riddle either. The barbarian spends his life struggling with the question of which is stronger—flesh or steel. As a boy his father tells him the story of giants stealing the secret of steel from the gods, then fighting a devastating war against them. Afterwards, the secret is scavenged by humans from the battlefield and thus men are suddenly able to wield the power of gods. This does not improve relationships in human communities and lands, however, as we can see in the advice of Conan's father to trust only steel blades, never people or animals. So he is raised with the notion that metal is stronger than flesh, a notion that is soon challenged by the boss villain of the story.

Enter Thulsa Doom (played by James Earl Jones), a serpent-cult guru who kills Conan's dad with rottweilers and chops his mum's head off, then traffics Conan into child slavery. (He also does some shitty things to Luke Skywalker in another movie around the same time.) Decades of further trauma turn Conan into an *Übermensch* who finally confronts his nemesis, who then tells him the secret of steel. 'Steel isn't strong, boy, flesh is stronger! What is steel compared to the hand that wields it?'

This is kind of true, but Doom is a guru after all, and gurus always fuck with our heads by offering a kernel of truth wrapped in bullshit. He demonstrates the power of flesh by having one of his followers kill herself on his command, and then crucifying Conan on the Tree of Woe. But that's not the power of flesh he is demonstrating—it's the power of wrong story to control the minds and bodies of lost souls, while gaslighting them by telling them how powerful they are!

In the end Conan never solves the Riddle of Steel, and neither do the filmmakers. They think the answer is that flesh is tempered by a lifetime of trauma and loss the same way steel is tempered by fire and ice, but that is the lie of rugged individualism and the hero's journey. It is wrong story. As Pete McCurley says, damage remains as a memory, a flaw in the steel, no matter how many times you heat it up and beat it out on an anvil.

As a kid I wrote my own wrong story around the Riddle of Steel. *Trust nobody. Collect blades. Learn to embrace pain. Endure your enemy and learn from him because the answer to the riddle lies in the weakness of his fleeting power over you. Wait until it fades, then destroy him.*

I have some different thoughts now. While I didn't find the true answer and the right story at the forge with you and Pete, I may have found it while making ground-edge stone tools. These are not the disposable knapped microliths you may be familiar with from your local museum, but the painstakingly grinded ones that were once used for centuries, handed down over many generations. Steel can do more, can be mass-produced quickly, can be faster/bigger/better and accrue glory to those who wield it. But that glory is fleeting—the steel is claimed by rust quickly and must be replaced over and over until your land and people are destroyed. This is the price of glory. For me, the answer to the Riddle of Steel is a heresy against progress that can never be embraced or understood in my lifetime. It's ridiculous, and impossible to apply to our reality right now, but here it is: *you need to leave the ore in the ground until you have strong enough story to regulate its use in the world.*

That's the mistake we made when we hammered our spear tip out of that invasion ship's keel bolt. We forged ahead without establishing right story first, so now we need to make our journey to return it to the sea. But us-two have jobs in the real world, and children with special needs, so we don't have time this year for that pilgrimage. There is no calendar space for driving to the east coast and using the woomera we were gifted to throw that spear back into the salt water, where the ocean can continue oxidising the wrong story out of it. We might have time for it next year, but for now we will just have to imagine how that journey might turn out, for the sake of our narrative and our passage through all these circles of hell.

Hither come us-two, the infernal boatmen, spear and woomera in hand. We stand on a troubled coastline, either side of Pete McCurley as the stinging wind whips salt and sand into our faces. I step ahead of you-two, carrying that evil spear over my shoulder as I stumble a little in the angry, foaming breakers and set the end of the spear into the hook of the woomera with shaking hands.

'Throw it, throw it in now!' Pete screams.

I falter a moment, but then regain my balance and my body tightens with abrupt expectation, slowly ceasing to shake and becoming steady as a deep and sure sense of resolve settles over me like a warm liquid. I turn to Pete and his eyes widen in horror as my own narrow in a sly smile.

'No,' I hear my voice rumbling. 'It's mine!'

Us-two back away from the beach while Pete falls to his knees and screams at the sky in frustration. We hurry back to the estuary and climb into the canoe, which is now battered and stained from our long journey. I climb into the front now, after shoving you into the back and throwing you the paddle. Did you think I'd paddle you like Miss Daisy through all these circles of hell? Fuck that. Row, you bastard! I got this *purri* spear now and I'm giving the orders!

Suddenly, an iron-rich spring extrudes from deep in the earth beneath the estuary and hits the water, oxidising and changing colour to sweep outwards in a lurid, scarlet tide, and now the river roils like boiling blood. You paddle through it towards the land where those who were violent in life make their home, and I start laughing like the devil himself while Pete yells something from the shore. It sounds urgent, but we can't quite make out the words—something about a wrong path.

You're It

There are three areas to explore in this circle of hell, but we're going to stay in our canoe and boycott the place until they let all the sodomites go. Brother Dante has some silly ideas about equating gay love with violence, and eventually I'm going to talk him out of all that. Until then, he can shove his seventh circle right up his second circle. While we wait, we might stretch our legs on the bank and play a game of tag. Stay away from the trees, though. There's harpies in there who like to nip from time to time, and I can tell you it stings.

Tag is a universal game in this world, but in Aboriginal Australia the rules are quite different from the non-Indigenous version. In European cultures, being tagged and becoming *it* means you have been infected by something and you are compelled to pass that contagion to others, either to relieve yourself of the burden or to infect as many players as possible until everyone is *it*. In the Aboriginal game I'm familiar with, however, *it* confers the agency of being able to run towards the other end of the field and score a point by crossing the line. You gain that agency by tagging somebody else who is *it*, taking that power from them and running as far as you can before somebody from the other team tags you and starts running the other way.

I've never seen the game conclude with a clear winner or loser, because kids tend to get lost in the joy of it and forget the score. They also keep forgetting which team they're on. The game is lightning fast and *it* changes hands every few seconds, with no single person ever holding or lacking power for too long. All the players on the field swirl and dance in emergent, self-organising patterns, like birds flocking or fish schooling. The game is violent and noisy, but nobody ever gets injured. It is beautiful.

I've raised enough children to adulthood over the years to be convinced that distinctive patterns of violence in both Indigenous and non-Indigenous worlds always seem to be reflected in the games our children play, whether it be tag or cowboys and Indians.

The restricted role of violence in traditional Aboriginal Law is something we struggle to maintain today for the health of our communities, but this Law is incompatible with the competitive dynamics of the game of empires that is played across every inch of this planet's surface. There are no self-organising, distributed systems of power in this global contest, only a minority of winners and a majority of losers. These rivalrous, murderous games find their way into every boardroom, every playground and every living room, including the most intimate domestic spaces of our own Indigenous families. Still, wherever possible, we continue to assert our relational approach to conflict, which can resolve things beautifully from time to time.

The other day I caught a taxi to the airport. The driver was belligerent and suspicious of me, and he smelled of horses, but not in a good way. It was that particular scent that could either be stale horse sweat or Tuesday's underpants on a hot Friday afternoon. I gave him the benefit of the doubt and decided that he was a horse man.

After a while I was silly enough to take my jacket off, revealing a T-shirt with Aboriginal designs printed across the front. The driver glanced angrily at me a few times in the rear-view mirror, then asked me if I was Indigenous. When I said yes, he pulled over and demanded that I pay the full fare up front before continuing. In the competitive game of this empire I have to live in, I had a few moves to choose from at that moment. I could have walked home, or punched him out and gone to jail, or filmed him and posted it online, or taken his name and number and tried to get him fired. But all of those options would have turned him into a bigger problem to inflict on others in the world, so I chose to follow the best option my culture afforded me— making a relationship with him.

It was a long cab ride, so I got him to tell me his stories and then shared mine and made him laugh a bit. I recounted the shocking colonial history of my community in a very compelling elevator pitch, and he cried a little, then while he was emotionally vulnerable I set about completely radical-ising him. (Yes, that's just guru trickery, I know, but it was for a good cause and there wasn't enough time for anything else.) When I got out of the cab at the airport he drove off with his fist in the air, calling out the window, 'Land back!' Weirdly, that made me want to punch him even more, but my heart seldom follows my head in these matters, so I just ignored it.

I'm not suggesting I belong to a culture of non-violence— far from it. It's just that when you remove the rivalrous dynamics of civilised economies, there are more options available and conflict becomes a power that is shared, distrib-uted and productive. In our old ways, if the driver kept being a prick we'd pull over and punch-on for a while until we came to an understanding. The fight would be intensely rule-governed and neither of us would be hurt too badly. It would not be about establishing a dominant 'winner', but about both expressing our grievances explosively, getting it out of our system and then walking away with our dignity intact and a new, mutual understanding of reality to share.

This is not unique to Aboriginal culture. No matter what your ethnicity is, if you were to ask your great-grandparents about fist-fighting in the old days, chances are they would tell you the same story. Choking people out and stomping on their heads is just not normal behaviour for humans. There's worse too—a young relative of mine recently threatened to 'skull-drag' somebody who had insulted me online, and when I looked up what that meant I nearly threw up. Where do kids learn this stuff?

Dignity, mutual care and respect are our default settings as a species. Like most mammals, we must also carry the capacity for violent struggle, but that has to be limited by good governance and never held by one person or one group exclusively. It must be accessible to all, moving from actor to actor constantly, just like the Indigenous version of tag. Any weapons used must be beautiful, for display as much as defence, and must be limited in their potential to do large-scale damage.

Most of these pre-colonial martial arts have been stamped out and forgotten, or only survive in fragments today. I'm ashamed to say I fumbled the opportunity to learn my clan's martial art from the last old man who knew it. He had agreed to teach me but said I had to learn how to make a shield first. I was working and raising several children at the time, so it took me a year to learn shield-making in my limited spare time; when I was finally ready the old man had passed away.

I've spent years since then finding fragments of technique from different Indigenous communities all over Australia, then patching them together over the whole cloth of martial-arts systems from overseas. It's a work in progress and I can't imagine any situation where I would ever use these gentlemanly skills, but for me it's mostly about discerning principles of governance, social dynamics and distributed justice systems that might be applied to communities in the future, as we all transition back to healthier ways of living together in this world.

There is a lot of posing and posturing in our old combat systems. If projectiles are in play, you strike a pose that makes you smaller, crouching behind your shield with a cocked leg, coiled like a snake about to strike. Have you ever seen the eyes of an animal cornered or defending its young? You put on those eyes, which are extremely unsettling. If hand-held weapons are being used, you strike a pose that makes you appear bigger. You bring fire and stone into your eyes then, and it all looks very impressive.

The only problem with this system is that it is not terribly useful for defeating enemies, because there are no sudden or sneaky strikes—you mostly telegraph your more powerful blows, often from an exaggerated high-guard, because the aim is not to kill each other but to have a spectacular battle.

There are angry dances to do before and during the fight, performed by both spectators and combatants.

I've spent the last year learning a bit of Escrima, a system from the Philippines where you fight with two sticks. I'm not very good at it, but I've found it's been useful for my thinking; coordinating opposite movements with two hands seems to facilitate neural connections that improve my ability to analyse complex or incomplete datasets. I made two thin but heavy *gidgirr* clubs from our own Indigenous designs to train with, to slow my movements and also try to get some muscle back into my flabby, Covid-lockdown arms. Once I had mastered some basic patterns, I switched over one of the sticks for a shield and spent time dancing and moving until some old patterns began emerging from my ancestral memory. It's not something I will ever perform for people—it's there to help with my thinking about what can be retrieved forward from our old ways that might be of service to the world in the present and future. As always, the wisdom is not in cultural things, but in cultural processes and protocols.

I can't really continue with the Filipino martial art, though. For a start it feels weird to learn it without standing on the soil where it comes from, learning the languages there and coming into right relation with the people who own the discipline. Also, in my community, dual-wielding two sticks is a combat system that only women can use. As with many elements of our culture, fighting styles are divided into Men's and Women's Business, and I have to say the fragments I have encountered of women's martial arts in Indigenous Australia are incredible. My colleague Debra Dank owns a centuries-old women's fighting stick, and recalls seeing female Elders fighting with them when she was a little girl.

'Back then, the grannies almost danced as they took turns hitting each other on and around the tops of their arms. Their movements were guided by rules decided long ago, for how to correctly fight with a stick—no one moved out of the way of a hit, certainly neither dodged, and each took their turn in the right order. They were both honourable, Law-abiding women and fought as Wakaja and Gudanji women had always fought, holding their sticks the right way. I think it was assumed that if you were ignorant enough to not know how to hold the stick, then you deserved the inevitable smashed fingers. The heavy hitting continued and, each time an arm was hit, exposed breasts would shudder with the shock waves travelling from the stick through the body. I'd sat with the other kids and watched and with every hit, the echo travelled through the ground and rattled my bones. The grannies fought on for such a long time that it was surely only the momentum of their measured back-and-forth stepping rhythm that enabled them to remain standing. I don't know why they had to fight but I know there was trouble over someone taking a perentie when the Law said it should have been someone else's goanna.'

Look at those grannies go! Martial arts is everybody's business; always has been and always will be. Some people might think there is no place for physical combat in a techno-utopian future, but they need to be aware that the tech bros who are building their digital paradise are obsessed with Brazilian jiu-jitsu and mixed martial arts. They are drawing on the philosophies and testosterone-fuelled ethics of those sporting communities with every line of code they write. Meanwhile, crypto-fascists 'just asking questions' online are also recruiting from these fight clubs, then acting the quiet part of their politics out loud with street violence and armed public gatherings. And none of them give a shit about their grannies.

I yarned with my friend Arpad Maksay about the phenomenon of Web 3.0 thought leaders and decentralised-automated-everything gurus building their workplace cultures and new digital systems around the most aggressive forms of new martial arts available in the manosphere. (Manosphere is the term for boys-only online communities that don't work and play well with others, especially if they're female.) We both agree that we seldom talk to tech bros without them soon turning the conversation to their martial art within quite a short time—unless there's a female in the room.

Arpad is the son of a Hungarian father and a Tamil mother, raised and educated in Australia and now working in marketing in Copenhagen. He has achieved

6th dan in kendo, the Japanese art of sword-fighting. He and his colleague Dr Kate Sylvester once ran a kendo corporate-retreat program for tech firms, ensuring that both male and female executives could share some common martial-arts metaphors and philosophy while creating digital systems.

Kate has the same level of mastery as Arpad, and as a coach she took the Australian team to third place internationally. Arpad says Australian women's kendo is stronger than men's kendo by any measure.

'What I love about kendo is that the armour and bamboo sword levels out brute force as a decisive element. Men and women train together and as a man you are certainly going to find yourself in the position of being defeated by women and girls from day one of your training, which you will not experience in a lot of other sports.'

He thinks it's useful to introduce this discipline to the tech community, because at the moment the dominant forms embraced by tech bros are mixed martial arts and Brazilian jiu-jitsu. I would bluntly categorise these as strong-man forms grounded in strong-man philosophies that induct males into strong-man politics. Online communities that have turned these martial arts into dick-centred disciplines are hotbeds of radicalisation for anti-female hate groups and the usual constellation of conspiracy theories and proto-fascist movements that have metastasised throughout the web.

I know this because many of these men follow my work to cherrypick savage factoids for their project of transforming themselves into indestructible cavemen. 'Savage' is a word they use in place of 'cool' or 'awesome' and they like my rough, no-bullshit voice. I know them because I spend a lot of time talking to them, and I'm only a couple of memes away from becoming one of them myself. Is it possible that this cult (and it is a cult) might alienate and sideline women in tech workplaces or online who aren't nerding out on the same approach to physical activity and competition?

In our yarns, Arpad and I speculate that the predominance in the tech-bro community of martial arts in which size and strength confer advantage has the effect of excluding females from key conversations in which the culture of the tech space is created. Considering the number of times we've heard these men reciting 'facts don't care about your feelings' stats and studies about physical and cognitive predispositions of males and females, I think there is a correlation to be found here. I'm not sure these cultural mechanisms of exclusion are consciously planned, but they can emerge from the collective desires and confusions of a massive population of fellas who have no-good relationships with women. And fascist gurus know that there are always useful idiots to be found in any gym or fight club.

Arpad thinks kendo can solve all of these cultural problems, including the competitive dynamics of a marketplace that constantly demands faster/bigger/better. He says the discipline tempers aggression because in order to attack you must first achieve harmony with your opponent. You must connect and flow together, then disrupt that flow in order to create the opportunity for a blow. You cannot strike effectively until you have come into relation, not just with the person you are facing, but with the genealogy of the discipline and with the sword itself. Maybe that is the true answer to Conan the Barbarian's Riddle of Steel.

There is *satsujinken*, the killing sword, and then the higher form of *katsujinken*, the life-giving sword. The first makes you feel taller by cutting others down, while the second is about improving together. Arpad says the art is so anti-competitive that kendo organisations are actively resisting efforts to make it an Olympic sport. With the perverse incentive of Olympic gold, nobody would be willing to risk anything in the vulnerability of relatedness. It would become preferable to attempt an easy victory won with half-points through cheap, nasty little thrusts and cuts. The combatants would be dancing against each other rather than dancing with each other and the soul of the discipline would be destroyed.

However, I'm not entirely convinced that kendo is an ideal solution to the gender gap in tech. I'm endlessly enraged by 'girls in STEM' (Science Technology Engineering Mathematics) programs with approaches like, 'Hey girls, you can use science to take better selfies!' but if the only

206

other alternative is, 'Hey girls, pick up a sword or go home!' then I don't know what I'm going to tell my daughters.

Kelly Menzel, an Aboriginal colleague from the Adelaide Hills, helped me navigate some stories about gendered violence in my previous book, *Sand Talk*. Together we challenged the 'when we were cavemen' myths of women as gatherers and nurturers and men as warriors and hunters, wrong stories that dominate a lot of contemporary science around sex and gender. This was an empowering alternative narrative for many women, but on reflection we were concerned about some of the implications of our logic. If we assert that women for most of human existence have not been passive victims of male violence, but rather have been formidable beings with considerable agency in physical conflict, then the extension of that logic might be that if contemporary women are victims of abuse, then it is their own fault for not learning how to fight better.

This didn't sit well with us, so we spent the next three years working on a research project to find a more nuanced understanding of contemporary violence. Our words had made a mess in the world for women frequently referred to as either Karen or Becky, and the Law of our culture demanded that we clean this mess up. So we began a research project about physical conflict between colonists, to discover a more nuanced understanding of settler violence and what role (if any) gender might play in the way it is enacted in the world. (Spoiler alert—it made things even worse.)

Our theory of violence was that most contemporary community conflict is probably dysfunctional, resulting in damage to relatedness. There is public violence and private violence. Private violence (domestic abuse, family violence, punitive beatings, sexual assault) results in the most horrific damage, is not transparent and is not rule-governed. Public violence (sporting events, street fights) is transparent but is likely to cause damage when it is not rule-governed. However, public violence that is rule-governed may play a vital role in increasing relatedness in communities.

We engaged in a kind of 'reverse anthropology'—two Indigenous scholars studying settler-on-settler violence, working with a dataset comprising online street-fight videos from six different colonies. We had read too many traditional anthropological studies of Indigenous violence in which conflict had been instigated or escalated by researchers in order to support social Darwinist dogma, game-theory models and selfish-gene hypotheses that were then deployed to justify free-market ideologies. We did not want to replicate the same kind of academic violence and produce the same kinds of social externalities. So we set out to conduct the study in a way that would increase respect, relationality and shared narratives.

To this end we employed a groundwater methodology, which involves engaging with datasets in ways that mirror the thinking and relational processes of walking through the landscape and looking for things that are both seen and unseen—an embodied awareness affording a multifocal bird's-eye perspective of terrain. For example, to find groundwater, one might look at the growth patterns of plants, the flight of birds, the colour of trees or the direction of their longest branches, and the aggregate of these signals in a sentient landscape extending from and incorporating one's own body.

The method of inquiry is rigorous, requiring more than triangulation—we referred to it as 'polyangulation'. The branches of a tree may seem to be reaching towards a particular piece of ground, but are the other trees around it doing the same? Is the grass different there? Is the soil damper than the soil nearby? What is the bird sign indicating there? Where are the ridges in the topography of that place? What insect activity do we see in the bark of the tree? A plethora of indicators must align, along with a particular feeling in the gut while standing in that spot, before a consensus judgment can be made about the presence of groundwater. We approached the highly complex incomplete datasets of street-fight videos from different colonies with the same pattern of inquiry.

Each stage of data collection and analysis utilised different forms of cultural expression and inquiry—visual practice, land-based practice, material-culture practice, spiritual and ritual practice. We undertook cultural activities using two sticks containing data recorded while viewing the street-fight videos over four weeks, examining the data at each stage with a different focus—connectivity, diversity, interactivity and adaptation. Data were not recorded digitally, but as notches and marks (number-story/quantitative) and symbols (picto-story/qualitative) drawn on those traditional weapons.

The number-story (quantitative data) was recorded on a woman's fighting stick of *gidgirr* wood and the picto-story (qualitative data) was recorded on a man's fighting club made from English walnut. European wood was chosen for the qualitative data-collection phase, as it was anticipated that some images may be problematic and inappropriate for carving on an Indigenous Australian wood, and we also wanted to pay our respects to the entities of land in the distant nation that is currently exerting illegal sovereign power over our unceded continent.

The settler street fights were evaluated according to Indigenous criteria of rule-governed violence—combat designed to increase rather than damage relatedness. The criteria were established from a literature review and community consultation, outlining four boundary protocols and four cohesion protocols for healthy public violence.

BOUNDARY PROTOCOLS:

- No hair-pulling, kicking or continuing on the ground, and no use of weapons
- No serious physical harm—have to be able to walk away

- No collateral damage to non-combatants
- No unfair fights—consenting agents, combat limits ensuring equal participation

COHESION PROTOCOLS:

- Maintain dignity of everyone present
- Seek resolution and coexistence
- Relational accountability beyond the interaction
- Group governance—adherence to a code

One hundred videos were viewed from six different settler states: Australia, Canada, Israel, New Zealand, Taiwan, USA. For each video we recorded and analysed violations of the Indigenous boundary and cohesion protocols.

The first category of Indigenous protocol violation was dirty fighting. Dirty fighting was categorised by actions such as hair-pulling, ripping clothes, striking a fallen opponent and so forth—basically any violent act that did not involve standing and striking an aware opponent. We relaxed the Indigenous protocol against kicking as we recognised this as a cultural difference in fighting styles that deserved our respect and tolerance. Kicks to the head and groin, however, were classified as dirty. Seventy-six per cent of the observed street fights contained elements of dirty fighting.

The second category was intentional harm, which consisted of any act that was clearly intended to damage participants in a way that would require more than an overnight stay in hospital. Seventy-three per cent of the videos contained acts intended to significantly harm or maim combatants.

The third category was collateral damage, involving instances of combatants losing control of the fighting space and either intentionally or unintentionally harming onlookers or passers-by. Fifty-five per cent of the fights contained incidents of non-combatants being harmed or assaulted.

The fourth category of violation involved the Indigenous protocol of 'fair fight'. This is difficult to define but involves mutual consent, cohesion of intent for both combatants and onlookers, and a general adherence to most of the other protocols being measured. Fair fight is more than the sum of these parts, ensuring that all participants will derive some kind of benefit collectively and individually from the shared experience, not at the expense of victimising and alienating a participant. Combatants don't need to be evenly matched, but there must be a reasonable chance of a fighter being able to give a good account of themselves. The relative size and skill of combatants can't be too asymmetrical and there must be a sense that justice is being served. One-third of all the fights viewed were classified as fair fights. Although this vague protocol is more prone to confirmation bias, it should be noted that we were pleasantly surprised by how many of the fights were fair from our point of view, as we had extremely low expectations in this category and had to revise our assumptions about the lawlessness of settler violence.

Dignity was the fifth category, a protocol ensuring the autonomy, reputation and spirit of all participants (including onlookers) is not damaged by the violation of social norms or the loss of control and integrity. There is a sense in this protocol of a person retaining their self-determination and awareness while also fully expressing their passions. Sixty-eight per cent of the fights contained violations of the dignity protocol, with participants compromising their own dignity or diminishing the dignity of another. This figure would have been higher if our ethical protocols had not prevented us from including videos depicting shamefully excessive levels of indignity. We were careful to show respect to the fighters in this way, and immediately stopped viewing any fight that resulted in degrading conditions such as involuntary nudity—a sample selection criterion we called the butt-crack rule.

The sixth protocol of responsibility and coexistence was measurably present if participants demonstrated a sense of belonging within a culture or community and adherence to the values of their culture, specifically that participants were 'fighting for' the maintenance of their collective value system rather than simply 'fighting against' individuals in response to personal slights, or attempting to avoid responsibility for a transgression by 'kicking up the dust' through the unnecessary escalation of a conflict. This protocol was demonstrably absent in fifty-eight per cent of the fights.

The seventh protocol, closely aligned with the sixth,

was about relationality and accountability. The main difference between this and the previous protocol was time—not
just a sense of responsibility during the fight but that there
would be accountability for transgressions following the
fight. Accountability to state institutions (such as police or
mental health services) did not count for this protocol. There
had to be evidence that the participants existed within some
kind of relational network together in their community
and would be held accountable within these relationships
following the fight. In fifty-seven per cent of the fights this
protocol was very clearly absent.

The eighth protocol was governance, which was deemed
to be present if there were any attempts made to establish or
enforce rules, or if any participants took on the role of adju-
dicating or attempting to break up a fight. The majority of
the fights contained evidence of this protocol being upheld
to a greater or lesser extent, with thirty-eight per cent of
fights being deemed completely lawless.

We noted that outsourcing governance to state institutions did not work in any of the street-fight videos in our
dataset. In fact, in every case where police were present, the
violence escalated to extreme and lawless behaviour, and
community governance ceased. Several of the fights began
only *after* the police arrived. We saw no examples of fights
de-escalating with police intervention.

We found that there was a strong moral code clearly
present in settler-on-settler violence, although this was

frequently violated when individual and social pathologies arose, indicated by disruptions to relatedness (such as over-consumption of alcohol, extreme narcissism, group hysteria, assertions of white supremacy). There was a measurable presence of behaviours that echoed most of our Indigenous cohesion rules. We began to perceive these rules as existing beyond the Aboriginal community, as a kind of social technology common to diverse human cultures, assisting with the maintenance of self-determination for both individuals and collectives, thus creating a generative tension and balance between autonomy and relationality.

While we saw that these behaviours were patterned on different cultural norms from our own (chivalry, gender-identity expression, domination), we respected them as enactments of valid customary Law in settler communities. This respect enabled us to take note of the instances when those demotic structures were absent and find variables in common across those events.

We discovered a significant comorbidity between extreme lawless violence and illegitimacy of the settler state. The more precarious the state in the international context (e.g. regional hostility or isolation, condemnation over lack of treaties and genocidal policies) the more likely it was that extreme lawless violence would occur. This was particularly evident in Israel and Australia, which were the only settler states where we observed firearms being deployed during street fights.

We were ashamed to admit we had expected to see firearms mostly in African-American communities, due to our lifelong exposure to American films and television. But we saw no firearms used in these involuntary-settler communities (even when a handgun was visible in a losing fighter's waistband) and noted our Indigenous cohesion rules were far more likely to be present there than in other US settler communities.

In all settler states observed (except Canada, where nobody seemed to take the fights particularly seriously unless hockey was involved) minority cultures were more likely to exhibit rule-governed behaviours in street fights. That is not to say that whiteness was the common variable here, as the mainstream conflict protocols observed in Taiwan's dominant culture were the same as those we observed in the other settler states. The dominant culture in every settler state showed the same patterns, including an enforced division in gendered roles, but this was most prevalent in Israel and Australia.

In Israel, women were mostly absent, even as onlookers. In Australia women were present in most fights, but their roles as cheerleaders or non-combatant peacemakers were strictly enforced. Australian settler women did on multiple occasions attempt to engage in combat, but in every case the male combatants would immediately stop fighting and work together to prevent female participation. Formerly passionate rivals, even in the midst of extreme rage, would unite as brothers and move together, in ways we observed as almost a collective organism, to separate female rivals either physically or through ridicule and sexualisation, or both. The ridicule usually took the form of violent, sexualised insults or catcalls, which universally seemed to have a depressive effect on the women, who became slouched, tearful and enervated, when moments before they had been highly motivated, energetic and skilled.

In one instance the women were clearly experienced martial artists (while the male combatants were not) and were instantly separated by a group of over a dozen males who had been fighting each other only seconds before. They deployed jeering insults of 'catfight!' and 'show us your tits!' while moving en masse between the female fighters. They bonded over their collective levity and ceased fighting, then began passing around beers and shouting jokes.

We felt quite enraged on behalf of those women, particularly when we realised the hopelessness of their position—that one way or another they would be policed into their designated roles. They could support, spectate, invigilate or intercede, but never participate in violence. We also noted that, in the majority of the fights, women were excluded from combat by their clothing—high-heeled shoes and flimsy or delicate garments.

By way of comparison, I also participated in a similar study led by non-Indigenous academics who were studying

Indigenous fight videos online. The study was almost identical, except that their ethics application was approved in a few weeks while ours took the best part of a year (there were concerns that we might end up portraying non-Indigenous people in a negative light). Another significant difference was the findings—the majority of the Indigenous street-fight videos contained female combatants, no significant physical harm was intended or enacted, and there was always strict governance in place, enforced by community onlookers.

It is tempting to draw partisan conclusions from these studies, but that's not the way science works in anybody's culture. These results are interesting, but they would need to be replicated and challenged a hundred times before they could be considered meaningful from either an Indigenous or western scientific perspective. For now, we're satisfied that we're conducting this ongoing inquiry with respect and integrity and that, over time, collective understandings on the topic may emerge that will be useful in the design of social systems that incorporate violence so as to increase rather than damage relatedness.

On the other hand, while it is a noble goal to act or lead in ways that are only informed by the best available research and proven scientific knowledge, contexts and realities are fluid and research takes years to do well, so that's only a formula for living today and planning for tomorrow according to yesterday's reality. Maybe we also need to be applying the best available methods and practices of inquiry in the moment, to live in a constant process of observation and analysis, with good ethical protocols that guide our decision-making as we go. And remember that anyone who thinks they have discovered the objective 'truth' is not only full of shit but probably trying to start a war (and sell you something while they do it).

In the meantime, us-two must accept that there is currently no correct way to say anything that will stay that way for long, and no comfortable or righteous way to be a pure ally or pure victim or pure bastard. In this chapter us-two have been all and none of these things. Good news, though—the minotaur of the seventh circle of hell wants to end our boycott, and has agreed to free the sodomites, except for a small handful who were also predatory lenders during the build-up to the global financial crisis. We're fine with that. He refuses, however, to stop using the term 'sodomite', but we'll fight that battle another day.

Everyone is impure and all states are temporary states, but still we must strive for right story, which in the end is the only game worth playing, although it's almost impossible to achieve. It's like trying to fall in love in hell.

So go ahead: you're it!

FIDELIO (OVERTURE)

A seed fallen on rocky ground struggling to take root,
a nut lying in a dark place sending desperate tendrils

towards a tiny crack of light—
these become the trees most beautiful, most startling,
most likely to remain after all other trees have fallen.

So too, beneath the pavements and monuments of
civilisation,
in the dark sites where dark money and dark ops
generate
unspoken and unspeakable cruelties,
where the souls of whistleblowers and iconoclasts are
thrown
to face silence and torments,
there are seeds of joy and liberty and love yearning for
the sun.

Every nation is grown from such foundations.

Regimes demand disappearances
and families search for their dissident loved ones
in printed records and mass graves.

Sometimes the lost are found in the liminal spaces
between paper
and dirt, in the dungeons of purgatory
where they mingle with henchmen, bureaucrats
and occasional bold interlopers in disguise.

You might hear them calling out from the long
shadow cast
by this monument of high culture,
gasping the names of others yet to be caged,

shrieking numbers that match the hidden tax on every
ticket,
the collateral damage of art, the songs of entropy
outsourced to the margins.

Yet even here romance is inexorable, and will sprout
against all odds,
and love will find its way,
wind its way through some hairline crack in the cold
stone.

When you see it, you may wonder if anything as
radiant could ever grow
from some sanitised paradise.

Drama, trauma, collateral damage and unrequited
longing make the manure
from which the most beautiful artifices can grow for
your pleasure.

Well, the seed has been sown,
as a woman moves now across that dark soil,
a woman whose lost love and desperation have not yet
eclipsed her wits.

She is lit from within
by foremothers who were once more than what she has
become,
a being severed from knowledge of the past and
enclosed by a stifling present,
with a precarious future lying ahead.

She is also lit by love, but will it be enough to
illuminate her way
as she commences her descent to the necessary
underbelly
of the great nation that both sustains and constrains her?

It remains to be seen whether love, once lost to that
frigid underworld,
can ever be retrieved.

Wrong Lines

Kek thul nungkaram wanttine'?

This question means more than its literal translation. My sibling seems to be inquiring about the physical location of my weapons, but he really wants to know where my mind is and what I plan to do to keep it on track.

Where's your spear and woomera?

The question is rhetorical and requires no response. It is often called out as a rallying cry, a challenge to stay true to the old ways and resist the seductions of civilisation and consumption, not to get too fat and complacent—your body and your knowledge may have to be put on the line at any moment to protect whatever vestigial sovereignty remains in your community. It's a celebration of brotherhood and survival.

It can also be a negative feedback mechanism to let a male know he is not meeting his cultural obligations, that he might be in danger of becoming assimilated. *Are you still with us?* It is a lighthearted jibe, but also a warning for a man to self-correct his wrong path. It has a lot of meanings in different contexts, but I know this is what it means for me today. I am, after all, on a strange hero's journey that began in a dark wood, where the right path was lost to me.

'Oh look, a mummy kangaroo!'

In the morning dew, an elegant marsupial is poised on the edge of flight, her dark eyes meeting our own and gradually calming, while something squirms in her pouch. It bulges and expands, until a pale horned head emerges, snarling, followed by a reptilian body that spills onto the ground as the grass steams and curls around it. The baby demon chews on the pelvis of a pick-up artist, while a torrent of snakes writhe past in pursuit of a hedge-fund manager. Horrors circle past us as we descend through concentric gouges in the dark rock, into something like a stadium made from the nightmares of a psychopathic cricket player. Hell is an open-cut mine.

Us-two are not afraid, because we have a strong relationship that is not just for mutual support but, more importantly, for rebuking each other when needed and steering ourselves back towards right path, right story. We do not praise and flatter each other as we pass through this infernal echo chamber, because we see what happens to people who do that down here, and it's not pretty. (I won't go into the details, but it involves a lot of *kaka*.) We will be a *memento mori* for each other—whispering reminders of our mortality and fallibility to stave off the excesses of our narcissism.

To avoid becoming trapped here, us-two will need to check ourselves and reflect on our hypocrisy. For myself, I have to recognise that I scorn others who claim to predict the future, yet I do a fair bit of that guru nonsense myself. I need to watch out for this behaviour down here, because the punishment for that kind of fraud is having your body twisted round until your tears end up falling into your own arse for all eternity.

Mostly, though, we will yarn about the fraudulence of innovations that initially seem helpful but are ultimately destructive, entities designed with good intentions but laden with ill intent, because no deep-time diligence (which is like predicting the future but without the bullshit) was applied to their conception. We'll also take a deeper look at wrong story as a psychosocial technology that informs the design of these innovations and justifies their unlimited production.

Wrong story has always been with us as human beings, but today it takes the form of public relations, propaganda and disinformation, at a scale that has become unmanageable.

It is the glove on the fist of technical innovation, providing justification for our worst excesses and putting enough dust and smoke in the air to prevent us from seeing the damage and acting on it.

To initiate this nauseating inquiry, I reverse-engineered the wrong-story process of unilateral innovation intended to increase the competitive edge of individual consumers, then dreamed up a new Indigenous weapon of mass destruction and built a prototype of this divisive tool, accompanied by some marketing packed with seduction and falsity.

Where's your spear and woomera?

My spear is at the door where it always is, but my woomera is on the fire in front of me, burning as I type on my laptop and the neighbours get wild about the smoke drifting across their properties. They'll be putting in complaints again, but there are worse things in the metropolitan air to worry about than a bit of woodsmoke. I'm burning the woomera because it's a wrong-story design that has the potential to destroy landscapes and societies over time. I made it unilaterally, outside of any communication with land and community, focusing exclusively on enhancing utility for individual hunters and warriors—a design process that always ends badly.

I carved it under controlled conditions, purely for the purposes of scientific study of course, and I have many layers of protocols in place to keep it contained. I'm pretty sure our lab doesn't leak. When I showed it to my

Indigenous colleagues in the lab, the first response was, 'Fuck me, brother. That thing makes me want to throw up.' I also showed it to my friend Adah Parris in the UK, a digital-spiritual guru known as the Cyborg Shaman. She thought it was beautiful. Then I showed it to an evolutionary biologist and he thought it was a good example of palaeolithic cultural development, a missing-link clue in the story of progress for hairless apes. But maybe they were just being polite.

Where's your spear and woomera?

The woomera is ash now, but weirdly still holding its original shape, waiting for a puff of wind or a jab from a stick to collapse out of memory. So I can study its shape and share what I learned from that wrong technology, while also knowing that it is already gone from the world. It's like I'm sitting with a fading ghost. I feel the same way about my work in an education system that is so often preparing people for jobs that won't exist by the time they graduate.

The major selling point of the wrong woomera would be the convenience and immediacy of multipurpose tools. The text for a snake-oil sales pitch might look like this:

My brothers, how often do you find yourself having to carry a parrying shield, digging tool, stabbing weapon, spear thrower, throwing stick, axe and club for miles and miles all day through the bush? How often have you groaned when these things need replacing, and you have to wait for the right season to travel to specific locations with kin to access the diverse materials needed for all those cumbersome tools? Do you chafe at all the ceremonies and activities you need to do in those places year after year to regenerate those ecosystems and maintain cohesion of community and land, your personal desires always delayed by the cycles of seasons and stars? What if I told you all of those tools could be combined into one new technology made from one kind of wood, sourced locally in convenient bush locations near your own neighbourhood?

Where's your spear and woomera?

We got your spear and woomera, right here! Say goodbye to all the messy family squabbles, the endless rituals, the frequent absences you have to take from your job, the regenerative land management and the burden of carrying half a dozen tools across countless hectares of scrub. Say hello to the Uptown Stick™—an axe, club, stabbing spike, spear thrower, shovel, parrying shield and deadly projectile all rolled into one easy-to-carry implement. It's convenient, concealable and upgradeable to suit your individual needs. With the Uptown Stick™, you can finally be free, independent and victorious in every fight! And you'll never have to leave town again! Here's a testimonial from a satisfied customer:

Before the Uptown Stick™ I was always taking unpaid leave from work for cultural reasons. I was often getting fired for frequent absences and penalised for my children being absent from school. But when I got the Uptown Stick™ I was free to hunt all year round close to town in the afternoons, after work, and that bossy uncle of mine finally got what was coming to him. The cheeky dogs on the beach side of town don't mess with me anymore. Everybody has an Uptown Stick™ now, and while kangaroos have become scarce in the area and homicides have increased, the upgrades and instructional videos give me a competitive edge that keeps me in front. I go where I want to go, and do what I want to do, and nine times out of ten I put the other guy in hospital. Thank you, Uptown Stick™, you've changed my life.

Recently I sat with a group of young wood carvers like myself, examining a collection of old wooden artefacts from around Australia. One of the patterns that emerged from these intimate group yarns was the way limitations are often designed into the affordances of our most deadly weapons to decrease the potential scale of damage in ritual warfare. An example is the awkwardness of tiny handles on large weapons—a massive sword made from a jagged sawfish blade or iron-hard rainforest wood looks like it could cut a man in half, if not for the minuscule handle that you'd struggle to get three fingers across.

This is the disappointing reality of truly sustainable design—it's just not sexy. The same weapon with a two-handed sword grip would be way cooler, but would also result in a chain reaction over deep time ensuring the culture could never survive more than a thousand years. It would trigger a self-terminating cycle of mistrust, advantage-seeking and competitive innovation that would first twist the culture and then slowly destroy it, along with the land-base in which that culture was embedded.

This is the difference between tech and TEK (Traditional Ecological Knowledge). TEK ensures innovations work over deep time, while tech ensures innovations work today and need competitive upgrades tomorrow. TEK only allows you to scale up your power, wealth and freedom to the limits of your relational obligations—the responsibilities you carry not only to your living relations (both human and non-human), but to your ancestors and descendants as well.

Tech is characterised by positive feedback loops without cultural regulation. TAP (Theory of the Adjacent Possible) equations devised by the theoretical biologist Stuart Kauffman best describe how this operates. In a system with a lot of potential combinatorials (relationships) in which two or three things might combine to form a new thing, there is a plateau for a long time where nothing much happens, followed by a sharp, explosive divergence of exponential innovation that completely changes the system. GPS + dating app + payment app = Uber.

Where's your spear and woomera?

In TEK, an equivalent theory might be proposed as TAR—the Theory of Adjacent Relations. The graphs emerging from this equation would show a gradual incline with less catastrophic phase shifts, as the humans caring for the system are operating in their unique ecological niche as a custodial species, intervening with minimal disruption to create regulatory feedback loops over deep time. The key to keeping track of stable innovation processes across multiple generations is story.

Story is a psycho-technology that can be more creative than a Cambrian explosion, or more destructive than a nuclear explosion. Story that maintains the continuity of creation requires a lot more work, however, and it develops over time from thousands of datasets held in relationships. This might be better described as a social technology. It never comes from an individual author. I've seen one emerging over the last few years, since the late sixties, from legions of workshops, self-help books and inspirational texts, tweaked more recently with an alternative ending that has arisen from engagement with Indigenous yarns in regenerative land and sea management and cybernetics. In a few decades it might become the seed of a good story, grounded in a real place with real Law and ceremony. At the moment, it is called the star-thrower story, and it goes something like this:

> After a freak storm on the central Queensland coast, a billion starfish are washed up on the beach, so numerous that you can no longer see the sand. They are still alive, but slowly drying out in the midsummer sun. A single man stands at the

waterline of the receding tide, picking up the star-fish one by one and hurling them out into the sea.

Another man wades through the windrows of dying echinoderms, laughing and shaking his head. He stops beside the other man and mocks him, saying, 'There are billions of these things. What difference do you think you can possibly make?'

The first man bends down, picks up another starfish and hurls it into the sea. He turns to the other man and smiles.

'Made a difference to that one.'

The second man nods, then picks up a starfish and throws it out into the water.

This is no longer where the story ends, however. Now an old Indigenous woman walks down to both of them and beats them around the ears with her stick.

'What are you doing? These crown-of-thorns starfish are an invasive species destroying my reef! The ocean tried to remove them with a storm and now you're throwing them back. Oh my god, that last one was a breeding female. You idiots!'

This is not the end of the story either. The liberated echinoderms may not have brains, but they are sentient and also have a place in this tale. They have nerve nets throughout their bodies and cognition that extends into their relations with the environment around them. This embodied cognition allows them to display some startling feats of learning, memory and problem-solving.

They employ this genius now and together

form a strategy for where to take refuge and how to repopulate. As they move together towards the reef, a research vessel captures them in a net and puts them in a tank to study.

The researchers are crypto-fascists and artificial intelligence enthusiasts, studying the starfish to help them develop neural nets for their bots, along with distributed networks for automated governance and decentralised finance. Suddenly the old aunty from the beach appears on the deck, and nobody knows how she got there.

'Where you going with those starfish?' she asks.

They tell her what they are doing and she gives them permission to continue, as long as they promise not to release the starfish back into the sea. She also says that they won't find what they're looking for through biomimicry research alone— they will also need to know starfish story.

'Aunty!' they cry. 'Can you tell us starfish story? Can you share your wisdom?'

'I don't know,' she answers. 'What does your grandmother say about your research?' she asks, pointing her stick at the expedition leader.

'I've never mentioned it to her,' he replies.

'Well, go tell your granny all about it, then ask her to come see me. If she approves of what you're doing, then I'll tell her starfish story.'

My friend Daniel Schmachtenberger, who works in the field of catastrophic risk analysis, expanded the story even further when I told him it was now a crowdsourced tale that resembled a free-range thought experiment. His addition went something like this:

> One of the scientists decided to tell his granny about his work on biomimicry-informed AI and to his surprise, this was enough for her to finally reveal the secret love affair she had with Johnny von Neumann back in the day. She also disclosed what he told her about self-replicating von Neumann machines, which he said could never be publicly known as it would likely end all life as we know it. Hearing this, the scientist was brought to a moment of apotheosis and existential devastation simultaneously as he realised his own research was on the right track for creating artificial life and consciousness, but that he now must also kill and hide his own findings forever.
>
> The granny and the aunty met and discovered that they had both known von Neumann, that the aunty had convinced him his invention must stay in the box forever.
>
> The scientist eavesdropped as the old ladies discussed the implications of starfish story, and he immediately called up a billionaire tech tycoon, shouting that he had the definitive answer for AGI and world domination, and wanted backing for the program before the Chinese figured it out first.
>
> The man on the beach at the beginning of the story has since started a non-profit for organising volunteers for large-scale starfish rescue. His TED Talk

has graphs about the starfish catastrophe and how we can solve it if we all work together. He is also prosecuting the old Indigenous woman for assault and battery.

The second man who joined in became an inspirational speaker and now makes seven figures telling this story to high schools and business leadership programs around the world.

There are some interesting messages in that seed of a story and 'white people are evil' isn't one of them, although it is always simple and comforting to retreat into that thought-terminating cliché. The messages that matter are about the unintended impacts of change-making and linear interventions, and the importance of context. The starfish themselves also have story that is worthy of respect and essential to understanding the contextual reasoning needed for any corrective actions in the land. The reef itself is also a sentient agent.

Where's your spear and woomera?

I was given an echinoid fossil by an elderly relative when I was a kid, one that she had found inland on southern freshwater Country when she was a little girl, where she lived as many people did in the late 1800s, in bark huts and tin shacks scattered across a dying landscape. She didn't know what the fossil was, although she thought she did. She told me it was a stone carved with magic symbols by an ancestor long ago. I had never seen a sea urchin before and neither had she, and I believed her. She was kind of right, in a deep-time sense, but not in the way she thought.

I still have that stone, which is the only tangible evidence I have now that my childhood ever happened, that the old girl ever existed. My memories are blurry, like they belong to somebody else, and I don't trust them, just like I don't trust the stories she told me. I just let them sit in the back of my mind, because sometimes they make sense when they connect with other stories. The bush skills she taught me certainly were real, because they still work for me today. I know she was real, because I still know where and when to find the eels.

When I was twenty-one, I had the fossil's pattern tattooed on my shoulder, as I thought it held the key to all the secrets of the old people, the secrets of life itself, so I still carry the mark of that ignorance today. Well, at the time it was a toss-up between that and a tattoo of Bill Cosby (on my neck, would you believe) so I'm glad I went with the urchin. It reminds me every day that my individual viewpoint on most things is necessarily grounded in ignorance, and I should never take my thoughts in any single moment too seriously, nor encourage others to do so either.

There is deep-time story in the echinoid, though, in the intelligent pattern its embodied knowledge left on that stone, and it has been working on me for a few decades now, driving me towards inquiries into distributed cognition and the way true narratives are created over time from an aggregate of viewpoints, including the ignorant ones. Those fossils are all over the world. In Britain, they call them faery loaves. Every viewpoint is ignorant, really, in one way or another. Combined over time, in right relation within and across generations, these diverse ignorances create right story.

But wrong story is unilateral and immediate; it does not stand the test of time. It is deployed as part of disruptive social technologies, such as propaganda and disinformation and dating-app profiles, to dominate and obscure the many voices that combine to make right story. Wrong story is an innovation that is placeless, with no map connected to any land. There are no songlines there, only wrong lines.

Where's your spear and woomera?

Around the same time I was given that stone, there was a bully at school who hurt me so badly that the physical damage he did continues giving me trouble forty years later. I still can't feel my shattered left nut, for example. The bully used racial slurs combined with homophobic epithets while he did his gruesome work (unavoidable when you're the only brown kid in the place and you like to read) but these things were just part of the language in those days and they ran over me like water, so his words didn't leave any marks and I can't claim that as some kind of bespoke trauma.

What marked me more than words or blows was the way others reacted to him, and the way he fitted so neatly into the institutional ecosystem of control, which continues to upset and disturb me to this day. The compliance and collaboration of staff and students messed with my head more than anything else. The bully terrorised many of my classmates but, for some reason I couldn't understand, everybody looked up to him and supported him as a kind of monarch in the mediaeval governance of the playground. The victims kept him in power, and I hated them for it even more than I hated him.

Most teachers tended to turn a blind eye to that kind of thing, perhaps because it assisted with the behavioural controls they had in place to keep students pacified and responsive to threats and rewards. One teacher wouldn't stand for it, though, and she put a stop to his psychotic attacks on the other students. She intervened and isolated him whenever he assaulted us, and things changed for a while. People began to talk and laugh together, sharing equipment and mixing outside of their cliques. Girls were playing the boys' games and boys were playing the girls' games and pretty soon there were just games. For the first time ever, it looked like I had started to make some friends.

But the bully knew exactly how to reverse that brief moment of anarchy in the schoolyard, that fleeting experience of a playground without hierarchies and categories and fear. He courted the veterans of the detention room and beatings in the principal's office, the boys who still felt the welts of the cane across their sticky palms and flea-bitten buttocks. He directed their impotent rage towards the anti-bullying teacher (who had actually campaigned to stop the principal from using corporal punishment), building a case against her as the architect of their woes.

He told them compelling tales about how the teacher was abusing and molesting students, tales that grew and grew until a critical mass of useful idiots held that wrong story as a true memory, and then spread it like a virus through the school. 'I'm not the bully,' he said. 'She is bullying me!'

The skinny boy who used to get beaten because he 'looked like a girl' became the bully's biggest supporter, proving his loyalty by inventing a story about the teacher abusing him and presenting this bullshit in a formal complaint. Police and outraged parents got involved. I protested and said the bully boy and his mates were lying, which was reframed as me bullying the bullies. My punishment for that was nothing next to the consequences the teacher faced. She was a single mother who suddenly had to struggle to keep her disabled son fed and sheltered, after she was sacked and lost her livelihood.

Life is more complex, however, than most subjective self-narratives allow, which is why I avoid them. I have a vague memory of looking on with glee and laughing when the teacher was sacked, then celebrating with other students when she was gone. I also put Epsom salts in her tea one time, to give her diarrhoea. Furthermore, I recall burning a red-haired kid in that class with a magnifying glass and calling him a ginger, which I'm pretty sure is some sort of racist hate crime. I was not some poor little angelic victim, although my inner narrator tells me that I am. While I was becoming a 'survivor' of bullies, there were probably others struggling to survive me.

I'm going to be really pissed off if I find out this was all a scenario like the film *Fight Club*, and I was the bully all along, beating myself up. Memories are shitty. I wish I were the hero or the victim in this story, but I'm neither of those things. The suddenly unemployed teacher was both, although I doubt that would ever have been of any comfort to her.

With all restraints removed and vengeance required, the bully pursued the reinstatement of his regime with extreme prejudice. And crushed my left nut like an egg. And the girls played the girls' games, and the boys played the boys' games and life went on as before. He's probably a CEO now, but I quite like the fact that I can't remember his name, or even his face. I'd probably think it was all a wrong story I'd made up in my head if I didn't still bear the marks of it on my body. The recollection sits alongside images of hot coals cooking freshwater mussels as long as my arm, and eels as thick as my torso and as long as a car. Those enormous things no longer exist today, but I'm almost certain they once did.

The echinoid story is true, because it is still there on my skin. I can trust that, but how can I make sense of it when it came from a traumatised old lady's misinformation? Trauma doesn't happen at the point of impact—it happens afterwards, if you can't find the sense and meaning of the experience. How can I make sense of the giant eels and mussels being gone from this world, so I can begin to eat the small ones again without the taste triggering a deep depression?

Where's your spear and woomera?

Writing about my personal stories always feels like I'm engaging too much in motivated reasoning and perception management, so I avoid it like the plague, but telling the land's stories always helps, and sharing that teacher's story has healed me a little.

She wrote me a letter once, but I never replied.

Stupid boy.

The narrative pattern I absorbed from that crappy school year was one I recognised again in high school, when I began to read about modern history and met children with Australian Nationalist Movement bumper stickers plastered on their lockers, proclaiming 'Asians out!' and 'Jews are ruining your life!' It was the wrong story known as fascism, and I can see the same pattern playing out all over the world today, more than ever. The teacher, that single mother who steps up for justice, is moments away from getting sacked and blamed for everything, and the bully boy and the fat boss with his flogging cane can't wait to see her gone.

I don't understand our longing for abusive dictators. It is a 'divine right of kings' narrative that's programmed even into the best of us. As for the worst of us—we long for the return of the king, an Arthur or Aragorn or Elon, a demi-god tycoon to maintain order and execute our enemies for us, to free us from regulation (but also impose iron laws on those unlike us, whom we despise but depend upon for our continued existence). We run that story on a loop in our heads and on our screens every day. Disinformation wizards use it to hijack our cognition, divert the frustrations of our oppression into support for the very systems and overlords who oppress us in the first place. Our rage is directed downwards and laterally instead of upwards, where it might be useful.

I know how this disinformation works, because that technology is fully installed in me now and has become a central part of my operating system. I personally generate at least two different conspiracy theories a week and I'm not even trying—it's just how my mind processes information now. This means I can't be trusted to make sense of it all. For example, when I see the same billionaires backing anti-vax propaganda who are also supporting the Big Pharma lobby to oppose price caps on vital medications, I can't help speculating that pharmaceutical companies would make a lot more money selling vaccines at a steep mark-up to individual consumers instead of mass-producing them for fixed-price government contracts, and suddenly I've generated a conspiracy narrative about Big Pharma being behind the anti-vax movement. This is how wrong story is born, with the best intentions and worst methodology.

I become concerned about my ideological bias, so I take that 'political compass' test online to see what my political brand is. No surprises: I end up as far as the test can measure to the bottom left corner. That would make me some kind of anarcho-communist. I don't like these arbitrary labels, though. It seems like there is disinformation right across the spectrum, with white supremacists marching alongside wellness influencers and New Age spiritualists, all following the same wrong story. Maybe we need a new way to categorise people for the purposes of understanding disinformation cults and those most vulnerable to them.

Aha! Introducing: the amazing psycho-technology of heuristics—ways of categorising things that are too hard to think about properly!

Here's a simple example. For convenience, we might say there are two kinds of people in the world. Here's a quick test to see which one you are—imagine the taps have been left on and your bathroom is about to be flooded. What do you do first?

a) Turn the taps off;

b) Shout, 'Who left the taps on?'

If you chose the second response, you could save the world by shutting up and staying out of the way for a while.

But see what I did there? I made a little heuristic, a little chunking tool for identifying a faction of narcissists who might follow me against an imaginary enemy faction and carry out my instructions, based on absolutely zero evidence and reasoning. You want me to be your flooded bathroom guru, don't you? If not, then you might be tempted by a child-trafficking narrative instead.

A child has been trafficked in your neighbourhood. What is the first thing you do?

a) Make sure the trafficked child is safe;

b) Express outrage about the trafficker and gather a mob.

There's a real limbic hijack in that 'save the children' narrative. That one is grifter gold. Who can argue against your position if you're the only adult in the room who is thinking (really loudly) of the children? Everyone in earshot can either be with you or with the child abusers. Yeehaa!

Where's your spear and woomera?

Wrong story is probably the most destructive technology in the world today, as it disables any efforts to mitigate any of the other toxic technologies that are being deployed out there. I have joined a research team and won a large grant to investigate it over the next few years, but until I filter my feelings about disinformation through some decent scientific and cultural processes, I may not be the most credible source on this.

That's another disinformation mechanism, by the way. 'Don't listen to me—I'm just an average idiot.' This is often deployed as a disclaimer for all the damaging rhetoric and disinformation that follows, absolving the influencer of any accountability. I guess the trick for us-two as we yarn through this book is to come into relation while also maintaining an attitude of open scepticism towards each other. Us-two should assume that even the idea of 'us-two' could be a trick, an illusion of intimacy designed to hijack our minds. But then what would that do to our relationships? How can we tell the difference between loving and love-bombing?

Wrong story is an innovation that eliminates trust and destroys social cohesion, whether it is consumed or resisted. Wrong story is fraud on a global scale.

Wrong story is a continually upgraded technology that shelters all the big planet-killing innovations that you are surely familiar with by now. It can take the form of disinformation's cousins: public relations, marketing and political spin-doctoring. It's the narrative that drives persuasive arguments for nuclear power as the answer to global warming, with belittling retorts for every challenge except the one question that matters—*have you figured out how to store radioactive waste without killing all our descendants yet?*

Wrong story told us that climate change wasn't real, then flipped completely and told us the solution was to push through by burning even more fossil fuels, because carbon makes more plants grow, and plants eat carbon, so all we need to do to reduce that gas in the air is put heaps more of that gas in the air.

Wrong story tells us climate change will trigger the

rapture and bring Jesus back. Wrong story gets us telling ourselves all kinds of bullshit.

Wrong story makes us fight battles to save the world by promoting renewable energy sources to continue providing the same (constantly increasing) amount of power to run the very devices and reckless innovations that are killing everything. It promises that these devices will become organic when the vast informational capacities of molecules are unlocked, harnessed and redesigned to serve our computational needs. But like rocks, molecules do that already, within systems that are incomprehensible to the people who want to strip creation back for parts and tinker childish functions out of the scraps.

Your smart home is not smart, not if the automated decision-making of a smart contract kicks in because you miss a loan repayment when your account is overdrawn to pay for your daughter's emergency kidney replacement, and you find yourself locked out on the street when you go to pick up a bag of clothes for her. Your smart phone can't help you either, when there are no humans in the central office to whom you can explain the situation, and a chatbot informs you that your family is now homeless.

Any affordance of every technology you can imagine is already provided as a function of your land, if you care to notice it and reconnect. The only reason to keep killing the land and upcycling toys out of its corpse is the desire to control it like a god, and then ultimately escape it.

Wrong story is a powerful innovation that works really well for a little while, almost like a superpower, but it is a fraud that will kill everything in the end—much like my wrong woomera invention. You're welcome to join me at the fire where I've just burnt that murderous tool. I can't tell you what to do or think, but I can tell you how much better I feel after putting that thing in the fire.

The hard part now will be walking my talk—trying to write the rest of this book without being a coercive prick. I'm not sure I know how to do that. I'm getting help, though. I have some good Elders and knowledgeable friends and family guiding me, so I might be able to see a way through the mists of despair and steer this canoe across a few more circles of hell with you.

Us-two won't be going on to ascend the mountain of purgatory like Dante did, though, because that's just Maslow's hierarchy of needs translated into deadly sins—a developmental model born out of the most destructive wrong story ever told (which we'll be looking at in the next, and final, circle of hell). We won't be exploring paradise either, as my muse is an Aboriginal woman. Megan won't be waiting around to inspire and uplift us, because she is a sovereign being who has her own things to do.

I saw a five-hundred-year-old copy of Dante's *Inferno* at an exhibition yesterday. It didn't look like it would last another five hundred.

Brother Ty, where's your spear and woomera?

Everywhere!

In our canoe we now have a tiny boomerang, a steel boomerang, a stone knife, a Lawstick, two clubs, the ash of an evil woomera, a problematic spear, and some fighting sticks we're dropping off along the way to people who need them.

Well, that was the plan anyway, until a bloody big giant picked us up and threw us down an icy well, where there's no exit in sight. This will be the end of our journey and you might be worried that we won't arrive at a resolution, that we might be lost forever with no hope of return. Don't look at me like that—I don't have the answers. I'm just the ferryman here.

Twelve Rules for Avoiding Lists of Rules in the Anthropocene

If your two spouses broke sacred Law and ate forbidden fish, betraying you and creation and everything you care about, would you pursue them in your canoe through lakes and rivers and finally drown them in the ocean as punishment? You might have no choice in the matter, because you have to fulfil that songline and make the story that will hold your descendants to the Law for all time. What if you found out that maybe someone had rewritten your sacred story a century ago, under the influence of Greek mythology? Would you still cast your spear into the sea and hurl your canoe into the sky in despair, then pass into spirit yourself?

Betrayal is an atrocious thing to deal with, whether you're dishing it out or receiving it.

We're up to our necks in treachery now, fragmenting our families and countries, excluding the visitors we've opened our doors to and biting the hand that feeds us, which for some reason has clenched into a fist. If your kinsman boasts about committing war crimes and you report him, who has betrayed whom? If your nation poisons the earth and water and you form blockades to stop it, who has betrayed whom? If the troubled teen you give shelter to is threatening your children and you kick her out, who has betrayed whom? If your guru gives you ayahuasca and then sexually assaults you to give you the gift of ego death, who has betrayed whom when you abandon his teachings?

Where is the Law? I want to weep but my eyes are frozen shut. Maybe this is a story us-two have to pass through to understand the why of things. The ancient Greeks wrote about a mythical icy land where the children of Apollo dwelt, a superior race living in a pre-civilised utopia. Maybe we'll start there, in that land they called Hyperborea.

Neither by land nor by sea can we find our way there, but we can see a reflection of that place beyond the north wind, butting at the glassy surface of the ice we stand on, redolent with the writings and murmurings of all the old Greek thinkers lingering half-buried in this frigid wasteland. Those ancient philosophers long for a return to pre-civilised perfection, finding it in tales of a mythical country without work, without disease or ageing, with perfect laws and justice for all, where everyone is exceptional and the weak or mediocre are not welcome.

These wrong stories of Hyperborea, a warm but snow-covered paradise occupied by a master race, arose from Greek invaders trying to make sense of the tribes they encountered while establishing northern colonies on Celtic lands and the territory of the Scythians, where Ukraine is today. They were astonished to find exemplars of human excellence in physical and intellectual endeavour in these tribes, people free from error and vice, living within lands so abundant that minimal labour was required for the provision of food, medicine and shelter, where men and women of leisure enjoyed equality, robust health and long lives in a world devoid of despotic rulers.

Opinion among Greek ethnographers was passionately divided as to whether these tribal peoples were virtuous supermen or depraved barbarians—a culture war that was invented millennia before Hobbes and Rousseau began today's pissing contest on the meaning of Indigenous existence. But all were able to agree on the myth of Hyperborea that was inspired by these encounters with the uncivilised Celts and Scythians. The scholarly factions united to create a fictional, utopian culture they could claim as their own tribal inheritance. The Greek aristocracy, displaying the utopian traits of leisure, abundance and robust health, could claim a more pure, undiluted genetic inheritance from these god-like ancestors, reinforcing their right to rule. Thus, the wrong story of Hyperborea was born.

As with most civilised religions and mythologies, it followed a Genesis story of an original earthly paradise, followed by a fall from grace and a long period of hard labour in service of a city, in order to push through to a time of apocalypse when there would be a reset to return all to a golden age of abundance and glory.

The Renaissance would later exhume and reimagine the Hyperborean myth, rebranded as an ancestral society of supermen known as Aryans. The desire to rediscover lost Aryan homelands, and other fantasy worlds such as Atlantis, would inspire much of the exploration undertaken in the Age of Discovery. In the 1800s, weird and wonderful artefacts, treasures and snatches of esoteric wisdom were collected from around the world and returned to the mansions of European aristocrats. There they donned turban, fez and headdress, inhaled exotic substances, cavorted in bohemian orgies, unwrapped mummies and held seances to commune with the dead. Gurus and grifters proliferated, employing spirit writing and astral travel to unveil the occult mysteries of human origins.

Helena Blavatsky was one of these grifters, emptying the pockets of the nobility while writing copious volumes blending western myths of Hyperborean and Aryan cultures with cherrypicked snippets of Buddhism and other eastern wisdom traditions. She built a cult known as Theosophy, grounded in an understanding of history as a cycle of great eras in which golden ages of superior races gradually devolved to degraded communities of former slaves living in egalitarian chaos, followed by calamitous revolution and reinstatement of golden-age rule, periodically Making Aryans Great Again.

Blavatsky established the idea of a taxonomy of human races, sequenced from most advanced to most primitive. You see, this is a developmental model where you improve and progress to the next level with each lifetime. Nations, as well as individuals, must all go through this process of 'development' and patiently await their turn to earn access to the privileges of nobility.

In the twentieth century, an Austrian paganist movement inspired by Blavatsky gained prominence among the plethora of occultist eugenics societies that were kicking around at the time. This nameless, amorphous, New Age cult fetishised runes and Viking symbols, spawning many secret societies seeking reconnection with Aryan occult practices from a mythic past. From this psychotic mess emerged the Thule Society, with members like Hess, Himmler and Goering, which then became a political party in Germany, and you know how the rest of that story goes.

They drank deeply from western folklore, Tibetan and Hindu traditions to expand on the mythology of an ancient Aryan super-race of tall, blond demi-gods possessed of superior biology and intelligence. Their claim was that

Germanic peoples were the inheritors of these genetic riches and would soon take their place as the master race of the planet with the dawning of a new golden age. They sought evidence of this Blood and Soil birthright through archaeological expeditions, linguistic audits of world languages and anthropological studies involving the measuring of skulls, to invent pseudo-scientific racial categories and taxonomies of human development.

This project didn't end well for them, and they finished up tainting the eugenics cult's brand for all of their followers throughout the western world. (And they were legion—even in Australia, if you are an Anglo person of middle age, there may be photos tucked away somewhere of your grandparents standing proudly out the front of their local Eugenics Society meeting hall). After World War Two, the master race could no longer be referred to as Aryan and had to be rebranded as Caucasian. This name came from the eugenics cult mythology of an Aryan mother-tongue originating in the region of the Caucasus Mountains. The troubling existence, however, of ancient Indian texts pre-dating western civilisation was creating too much dissonance to ignore, so an older pseudo-scientific history was exhumed to explain Hindu civilisations as originating in the west but fallen from grace, due to interbreeding between higher and lower castes.

It was a useful wrong story which had previously justified Britain's invasion of India as a humanitarian reinvigoration of the degraded civilisation of their long-lost cousins. This master-race theory was remastered to popularise the term Indo-European as a euphemism for Aryan. In the modern academic disciplines of anthropology, ancient history and linguistics, the original Indo-European homeland is often imagined to be in the region of current-day Ukraine. History doesn't necessarily repeat itself, but it certainly echoes when wrong story is replicated.

The eugenics philosophies that have more recently been labelled 'White Supremacy' have been cross-pollinating for over half a century with Hindu nationalism and Hindu fascism, escalating in recent decades through a cultural feedback loop from east to west, facilitated by various cults, including many schools of modern yoga. (Something to contemplate next time you find yourself in 'warrior pose', having your mind and body honed to perfection in preparation for…what, exactly?)

Beware of yoga instructors who get you to stay back after class to tell you that you're special. Same goes for wellness-industry influencers who are offering a similar brand of New Age developmental Kool-Aid. There is a reason so many yoga and healthy lifestyle devotees find themselves marching alongside white supremacists to 'hold the line' against the 'deep state paedophiles' and 'globalist banking families' (which is code for 'The Jews'). It's the same reason New Age spiritualists and crunchy moms stormed the US Capitol alongside Proud Boys and QAnon fanatics in 2021. Whether your Jesus is a Lord and Saviour or an ascended master who studied in Tibet, it's all one big happy family enjoying the same rune stones, crystal fetishes and wrong story.

Fascist and proto-fascist gurus in the west often draw on perverted blends of European and eastern mysticism to build their seductive occult ideologies. These obscenities form the basis for a lot of far-right extremist notions such as a glorious return to a golden age through the development of culturally exclusive and patriarchal ethno-states, anticipating the emergence of a god-king to lead them.

I met a man today who asked me the best question I've ever heard. I was expressing my concern that so many of these dickheads are reading my work and misquoting it in their appalling manifestos. He responded with a question that perfectly sums up my inquiry and my struggle in writing this book.

'What are the implications,' he asked, 'of giving your power, knowledge and tools away to people who misuse them?'

Ouch. I'm headed for the fourth circle of hell, to be tormented for my profligacy. My goal may be to share the regulatory mechanisms, ethical processes and cautionary tales of my life and culture to check the runaway destruction of our planet, but consumers of my work are under no obligation to use those tools for their intended purposes. Look at what the bastards did to yoga.

I think I have story for this, in the stone tool I'm currently working on for the writing of this chapter. I haven't finished it yet, because I've got another century or two to go before it's done. It's a story of restraint and patience that I hope you won't impatiently seize and start incorporating into your next personal-development workshop or corporate-coaching seminar. If that happened, who would be the bigger traitor, you or me? That's easy—you would just be betraying some trusting idiot you never met, which is no betrayal at all. I would be the idiot betraying millions of ancestors and the most ancient living tradition on the planet.

I am walking along a vast slab of flat stone on this southern beach. There are cliffs and a jutting extrusion of volcanic rock that looks like the body of a being fallen from the sky and buried up to his waist while he chomps on the heads of the damned. But the land and Elders have opened up to me, and they tell me a different story for this place. The water is freezing and so is the wind. If the earth was flat and I had a decent telescope I could sit here and watch Antarctica crumble into the sea.

The old people in this place are connecting me here and I don't want to hear their voices because I am still so vengeful and angry about the century of betrayals that have made me who I am. Still, they whisper, and I follow them along a crack in the rock. The tide is shooting water up from the shoreline through this ancient rut and a stone the size of two fists together shines out at me from its nest in there, where it has been jammed for centuries. It has the colour and sheen of living flesh, and it is smooth and glossy. I reach out and it is freed with a click, fitting my hand like it was made just for me.

Hundreds of thousands of tides have shaped it into a perfect hand-axe, and the edge is dull, but I could fix that with a few hours of grinding on the damp surface of the flat rock in this place. All my tools are here. I feel like this axe belongs to me, like the old people here have led me to it. I sing and dance with the sheer joy of discovery, but I'm checked by a surge of personal power and worth that I have come to distrust.

This is not my place. I have permission from Elders to work with stone and wood here, but still I hesitate. What do I know of the voices that called me here? I'm reminded of the endless lines of New Age true believers who have told me earnestly over the years, 'I was gifted this feather/stone/shell by the spirits of the land.'

I could take this almost-completed axe right now and finish it myself. Or I could put it back where it belongs and let the ocean keep working on it for a while.

I decide to give it another century or two. If any of my descendants find their way back to this place and make a better relationship with the land and community than I did, then they might hear the same call from the rock and sea, and pick this axe up. They will find ancient knowledge in there, alongside the cautionary tales I left in the stone about the calamities that arise from wrong story, and the perils of narcissism. I might be able to fool myself, and I might even be able to fool you, but I can't fool the land and sea. There's no ancient knowledge woo-woo that can withstand the scrutiny of place.

There are grifters everywhere. They make lists for us, or diagrams to help us navigate an increasingly complicated world in simplistic ways. Most of them are rubbish. Here's an example I made up, which has all the hallmarks of the guru grift—it has quotable memes, is a reboot of another successful list, and shows a developmental progression with an elevated state of being in the final step.

THE TWELVE STEPS TO RECOVERY FROM INDUSTRIAL CIVILISATION

We:

1. Admitted we were powerless within the current system and that our lives had become unmanageable.

2. Came to believe that knowledge and spirit of Country could restore us to sanity.

3. Made a decision to turn our will and our lives over to the custodianship of Country.

4. Made a searching and fearless moral inventory of ourselves.

5. Admitted to the Ancestors, to ourselves, and to another human or non-human being the exact nature of our wrongs.

6. Were entirely ready to have Ancestors, Country and Spirit heal us of these defects of character.

7. Humbly asked Ancestors, Country and Spirit to remove our shortcomings.

8. Made a list of all entities, peoples and systems we had harmed, and became willing to make amends to them all.

9. Made direct amends to such entities, peoples and systems wherever possible, except when to do so would injure them or others.

10. Continued to take personal and group inventory and, when we were wrong, promptly admitted it.

11. Sought through connection to Country to improve our conscious relationship with Spirit, Land and Ancestors, as we understood them, asking only for knowledge of the pattern of Creation and the power to increase relatedness within that pattern.

12. Having had a spiritual awakening as the result of these steps, we tried to carry this message throughout industrial civilisation, and to practise these principles in all our affairs.

A heuristic is a tool we develop to apply in complex contexts, a prefabricated set of instructions for dealing with problems and situations that are similar in different times and places. It can be applied to everything from self-help to policy design. To some degree this is necessary, because if we had to come up with a completely new approach for every problem, we'd never be able to feed and shelter ourselves. It is fine, unless it is grounded in wrong story. Developmental models are all heuristics grounded in wrong story, a Great Chain of Being narrative arising from the supremacy myths of empires.

Traces of their pattern can be seen across every pyramid-scheme model of development in existence. Can these models be saved if we change their shape from a triangle to a circle, or are they so hopelessly flawed by eugenics and hero's-journey myths that they need to be abandoned completely? That would mean eradicating somebody's culture, though, and I'm not too keen on ethnocide as a solution for anything. When I see people trying to decolonise their developmental models without eradicating their cultural inheritance completely, I can't help but have sympathy for their cause, although it may trouble me for reasons I am unable to express coherently.

A good example of this is integral theory, which has turned the developmental pyramid into a colour-coded spiral. Integral theorists read my work and tell me that I am one of them, and I'm not sure how I feel about that. I can't make sense of it through analysis, so I try comedy instead, and share my clumsy satire with them online. Some of them love it and some of them hate it, but I feel like it's the height of rudeness to challenge people's stories unless you can have a good laugh with them first and come into relation that way. It goes like this:

I keep running into this integral theory, which is right across the intellectual dark web, the meta-modernist movement and the booming coaching industry, along with every other corporate self-help program and sense-making community in the information ecosystem of Enlightenment 2.0. The founder of the system, Ken Wilber, seems to share my concerns that people are 'levelling up' through it like a game, or progressing through colour-coded stages like they're karate belts. Along the way they are forming castes and hierarchies of actualisation. I don't think it's what he had in mind.

The most basic expression of this developmental model is something like, 'Clean up, wake up, grow up, show up'. Plenty of gurus are getting a following by telling young people to 'Clean your room' which for some reason is a profound *aha* moment for many. Me, I say, 'Who the hell are all these people with their own rooms? I've *never* had my own room. Most of the people in the world don't have their own room!' And then I realise who the disgruntled target demographic is.

Anyway, there's more to it than that, and Wilber says that at each stage of development you retain the gains and understandings of the last, so at least the 'primitive' stage that I'm still in has something to offer for everyone, no matter what colour of consciousness they have achieved.

So I went to sit with the land, where the sweet underground water is still flowing strong, and I asked the earth what she thought about it all. I don't agree with everything she said, and she used some fairly inappropriate language, but hey, I'm just passing on the message.

Of course, she doesn't speak English, but a rough translation goes like this:

Clean up, wake up, grow up, show up? What's with all these ups? You want ups? Then shut up and listen up! Down is the way you need to look now. Slow down. Calm down. Scale down. Step down.

Slow down. Your life and 'development' are going too fast for you to manage all the knock-on effects and butterfly effects. Each solution, each hack, each fix is killing us all. Slow down. Listen to me. I'm down here, look at the ground, sit down, listen for a bit.

Calm down. You are too outraged about too much. Make room for other stories. Listen to people you don't like and see their wisdom. You all have the truth, but it's distributed, so you can't see it alone, only together. You can't do that when you're attacking each other, so stop it.

Scale down. Stop growing! Stop this bull-shit development! You don't need all this stuff, I got everything you need if you'll just live with me and work with me here. Your economy and financial system and supply chains are ridiculous and way too much hard work. Does everything have to be so complicated with you? And your personal development should be as easy as improving your relationships, especially your relationship with me. I am your mother, after all! And please don't go to Mars, I hate that bastard, and his fancy new blue bitch. I got custody of you now and you're staying with me. I don't want to hear any more about it!

Step down. Your power structures are unnatural and they're killing us all. If you are holding a boss-man position, please teach a team of younger people to take that on and distribute it productively throughout that group. You're not smart enough to hold that power on your own. You're a crappy boss and you're making a mess. There are younger people who could do it better, and many of them are my daughters. You shouldn't be making decisions unless you're young enough to have a feisty grandmother who can slap you and veto you when you get out of control. Step down, or I'll knock you down.

You see what I did there? I made another heuristic out of the bones of the one I critiqued. Development is inexorable, even when you actively resist it. I'm not sure you can even think in English without ending up in some quest for a unified, universal theory of everything. Development has roads that compel its devotees towards this quest, and no other. Why does this compulsion towards unification exist, when it can only destroy the diversity that makes up all of creation? Is it not enough to live and die, or do we need to develop the whole universe and take it with us when we go?

A few short years ago I was living on roadkill, collecting my meat on the road at sunrise. Now I'm getting fat on sourdough and quinoa while I type words into a void. Have I developed?

This reminds me of some yarns I had with my native Canadian colleague, Melanie Goodchild, about roadkill stories. She is an Anishinaabe systems thinker from the Moose Clan on Turtle Island. She says Indigenous systems knowledge represents an existence of irreducible wholeness, in which all things are in relation. She also says there is no native word for 'nature' as an abstract concept, but the word they use instead simply means 'everything'. Melanie believes that systems thinking is just *thinking like an Indian, like our ancestors did. And everyone has ancestors.*

We have been sharing turtle story together for a couple of years. Melanie carries a sacred object, a rattle made from a turtle shell, which is a big responsibility in her culture. Once she told me a story about running over a turtle with her car and what she learned from that.

She was travelling to a ceremony, passing a place where turtles cross the road, when she hit one and crushed it. She jumped out of the car and saw that it was a female with eggs, and it was dying. She was devastated. A week later she had a dream about a turtle walking into a lodge without a door and went to talk to an Elder about it. The Elder said, 'Oh, she came to you,' and Melanie replied, 'But I killed a turtle, this is just horrible.' The Elder explained that often spirit beings will give their life to you so that you can do your work. She said Melanie needed to connect with one of her sacred objects and the turtle helped her to do it, then showed her in the dream that she would be making a lodge to carry out her sacred work. Melanie then went on to help build a lodge that would become an institute for Indigenous systems thinking.

I shared with her a similar roadkill story, but one that never really amounted to the same kind of 'meant to be' conclusion. None of my stories has an ending like that.

For me, it was a white owl. The roadkill occurred after I was given a lot of white owl business to carry from a very senior Elder who identified me as having that Dreaming as part of my ancestral being, linked to a white owl and brown owl songline from South Australia to far north Queensland. She passed on a lot of that totemic knowledge, along with some skills that felt to me like superpowers at the time, because I didn't know any better. So I was carrying those new capabilities with me, excited and feeling very special and magical, when I heard a thump under the car and looked back to see white feathers swirling across the red dirt of the track. 'Ooh, no, no, no! I've ruined it! I'm going to lose it all!' I pulled up, tumbled out into the dust and picked up the owl's shattered body, rocking back and forth.

She wasn't dead yet, though. Her eyes were still bright, and she stared straight into mine with an intensity I've never felt before or since. Living knowledge passed from her eyes to mine, flowing like a river, as the spirit gradually faded from her. She uncoupled my ego from the knowledge the Elder had given me and installed it into every cell until it was part of my body and every relationship in my life. I understood I had not killed her, but that she had put herself in my way to turn those new skills and understandings into true, embodied knowledge. This was real, not subject to revision or opinion. It was an anchor for me, for a time, and I did some good things in the world.

It wasn't long, however, before another Elder found me and wanted that Owl Business for herself. I followed that guru for a few years, while she used me as a living battery and occasional hit man. Eventually, she asked for the Owl Business and I gave it to her. She could not make it work, though, and in a fit of jealous rage she threw a death curse at me.

I could feel myself dying from the belly out, so I tried to hang myself from a blackwood tree by a river. A dozen willy wagtail birds came and sat in the tree and screamed at me until I backed down and resolved to try and beat the curse. I did beat it in the end, but I was never the same again and today, when I call the white owls, they don't come for me. My spirit can't fly, and my eyes can't see shit anymore. Worse than the loss and worse than the curse was the Elder's betrayal of my trust. And worse than that was my own betrayal of my old people in believing her and throwing everything away.

I've drifted into what most people would call superstition

here, but this story captures beautifully the nuances of our topic in this final circle of hell: betrayal. It is tempting for me, as a sceptic, to decouple the story from my culture and dismiss it all as an extended psychotic break, but I won't let myself off the hook that easily, because this is right story even though it's unverifiable, and there are real-world things to learn here about spiritual treachery and existential uncertainty.

Beware the spiritual grift and the oh-so-shiny ancient wisdom of self-proclaimed shamans. Mostly it's bullshit, but sometimes it's outright dangerous. It's the worst betrayal, when all humans need spiritual knowledge they can trust, just as much as they need air to breathe. In a world where spirit has been colonised by cults, it is tempting to take refuge in reason, to the exclusion of all other knowledge. We do this because we need something to tether us to reality, but ironically the only things that do this well are superstitions and myths, because they inspire the supra-rational understandings needed to navigate complexity. We need right story more than ever as the world becomes less complex and more complicated, as it becomes increasingly difficult to know what is true, or whether truth even exists at all.

The idea that there is no such thing as truth is true, but it's only half-true. There's no such thing as one truth. For every right story there are a hundred other right stories that contradict it, and we need to be comfortable with that. If a thousand people stand on a moonlit beach, each one of them will see the moon reflected in a different place on the water.

'It's out past the breakers.'

'No, it's by those rocks.'

If they gather and share their truths around fires on the beach, they might arrive together at the conclusion that the moonlight is striking the entire ocean surface at once. But then, that would not be the end, because earth, sea, moon and people are still in motion and there is more to be known.

In *Sand Talk* I told a story about education, and it was true, but on its own it can only ever be wrong story. To become right story, it needs to coexist with opposite narratives that are also true, weaving a more diverse and robust understanding of history. The story went like this:

> Prussian scientists in the late 1800s invented public education based on the principles of domesticating and training animals, to create a population capable of forming nations—a new model of organising societies into massive countries of millions, alike in thought, word and deed. This would scale up labour to service the technologies and production lines of the industrial era, as well as creating soldiers capable of existing in permanent standing armies for the growing war industry. The system was founded on eugenics and proto-fascism, and was exported throughout the world.

Every fact in the story is verifiable and true, but the story itself is not right. It's nothing but propaganda. There is an equally verifiable story of public education being created for liberation, to give workers and minorities, no matter how poor, a dignified and meaningful life through access to literature, philosophy, arts and science. The goal was to create true democracies, which can only exist when there is an informed and educated citizenry with equal access to knowledge.

Every fact in that story is verifiable too, while also being contradicted by other verifiable facts in a thousand other narratives.

Like most educators, I've spent my entire career working towards a revolution in education, a change in the institution that might somehow, magically, produce a change for the better in our failing communities. Meanwhile, plutocrats have been commissioning automated machines and systems for education and training, not to improve the learning experience of students, but to mine their neurology for precious data. The students are still doing basic comprehension worksheets, not exploring universes of knowledge through miraculous devices (which they must hand over at the door when they enter the classroom).

Education tech is not for student development and improvement—it is for extraction and evaluation. Billions are invested into research and development for creating DNA-testing devices to find arbitrary genetic markers of more and less intelligent students, to sort them into social roles for labour from the age of five and stream them into different models of curriculum from day one. (At the same time, further billions are invested to lobby for lower minimum wages as well as lower age thresholds for labour and marriage.)

I have seen these AI prototypes proudly unveiled at seminars and conferences on the 'future of learning'. Meanwhile, we useful idiots from every kind of ideological cult wage wars against each other to battle over what kind of content will go on the worksheets. When the smoke clears, one team will indeed be victorious, and we will have our revised facts and fables, but the only real winners will be the plutocrats who financed both the culture war and the extractive tech.

Every revolution is a pump-and-dump scheme. In case you're unfamiliar with that term, it's when traders buy up lots of stocks to inflate the price so that every punter will jump on board and invest too. Then the traders suddenly sell, while their idiot followers lose the farm, at which point the pump-and-dumpers buy back the stocks again at a fraction of the price. This is the pattern of what empires do, and it is what they have always done. Those in the general population who have more privilege than others do not keep that privilege for long. They bleed in revolutions to enrich the powerful and reset their horrid systems for them, and in the end, we find we're all in the same canoe. We never remember, though, for the next turn of the wheel.

Decolonisation is good work if you can get it, but it is really just part of the pump-and-dump mechanism in which we all play our role. We don't have a colony problem, we have a decentralised empire problem. All of our resistance, support, organising, yearning and thrashing about with placards doesn't amount to much more than a warm feeling of superior morality, which the powerful aren't remotely interested in. They have fallen from grace and plummeted into the earth like asteroids, and they really don't give a damn.

The sand around that big jutting rock on the freezing coast is swallowing us now. We're sinking down deep as we scramble for handholds on that frigid body, and there is a river down there that sucks us into its serpentine form, drawing us against the current and inland. Our canoe and all our tools and stories are gone, and we begin to forget. We pass out of time and memory. There is nothing. There is no story and no truth, just a meaningless quantum soup that used to be existence. All is dark. Without story, creation can no longer exist.

Then a smooth floor. A hint of light. Shapes and a sunrise. We are in a supermarket, standing in an aisle filled with endless shelves of Easter eggs. Mammon has saved us, and Moloch offers gifts for our children, and we are not happy, but we are alive. This is wrong story, but it's better than not existing at all.

I don't care, though, because in the year 2222, us-two will go back to that beach. It will be warm there and we will dive in and swim down to that crack in the rock and pick up our axe.

And remember.

Little Birds

Us-two need to care for each other at the end of this journey, and I'm responsible now for making sure you don't walk away with more pathologies than you had when we first jumped into this literary canoe together. I'm not confident that all the wrong story we explored hasn't damaged you. I can edit out the worst parts before you find the book, but all the stories and relations from this journey still exist between us, whether you read about them or not. Things happened, and you were there.

So, what is the best science for me to apply here, where it matters the most? I don't want to be like one of those US

Senators who calls vaccines poison and invokes the power of prayer to win votes, but then secretly gets shots for his kids and mistress. I owe you right story here more than ever, story free of ideologies and other superstitions.

I'm a hypocritical atheist and that makes me an unreliable non-fiction writer. I'm a sceptic who nonetheless spends a significant part of every day collecting stray hairs around the house and flushing them down the toilet so a *purri* man can't find them and use them to curse my family. I'm comfortable spotting the fantastical bullshit in other people's spirituality, but I have a massive blind spot when it comes to my own. Even in situations where my way doesn't work anymore, I still persist with it. How about you?

If your back gave out completely and you could barely walk, you would be driven to investigate. Your relations around you would give and seek advice, which you would listen to respectfully and then act upon with all the agency you could muster. Us-two are the same in this, because it's how our species works. Human traditional medicine approaches diagnosis and treatment collectively—it has never been about outsourcing the entire process to a singular tribal shaman like they do in old books and movies, although medicine people with different skill sets are always consulted, of course.

How has this process been working out for you? It hasn't worked for me at all when it comes to chronic back pain. Relations are not just relations anymore; they are somebody's workers now, and they have little spare time for collective care. They need to demonstrate care, though, so hastily refer you to doctors, diets, products, gurus and treatments that have flickered across their screens recently. 'Listen to everybody' is my method, and it works in traditional Indigenous contexts but almost nowhere else.

My traditionally collective method has led me to consult people of many disciplines, including pseudo-scientific ones like rheumatologists, naturopaths and chiropractors, and these plastic shamans have prescribed everything from opiates and antidepressants to belladonna and ivermectin. Eventually I even tried scans and X-rays, which finally produced a sensible diagnosis—my back was broken and left untreated in early childhood and now it's basically stuffed.

From a holistic medical perspective, this pathology sits alongside a number of interrelated conditions from that time in my life, like foetal alcohol syndrome, persistent untreated bronchial pneumonia, otitis media resulting in permanent hearing impairment and a suite of other ills adding up to a shortened and unpleasant adulthood, caused by everything from cheap shoes to lead poisoning from camps around mining sites. No vertebra grinds itself to dust in isolation, and there is always a historical context if you seek to understand and mitigate a problem.

That's pretty much the limit of holistic inquiry for a spinal injury, though, if you only interact with human beings. But there are additional datasets if you wish to include those voiced by non-human participants. Of course, in isolation these data can only demonstrate correlation rather than causation, and cannot be reasonably verified or falsified. Yet they might assist with meaning-making around your condition, as long as we avoid trying to generalise 'miracles' at scale.

A medicine woman who recently put my spirit back into my body after it was displaced by a cheeky vertebra made that error in causation, so of course the ritual did not heal my back as she claimed, because the busted bone just kicked the spirit out again after a few days. There is magic in the world, but it doesn't scale or generalise, and anybody claiming they can work it beyond local, small-scale practice is full of shit.

The magic is in the world, and you can't manipulate it, but merely move with it in ways that direct you towards systems health. Through ceremony and ritual practice that aligns us with reality, we can supplement magic. Magic can't supplement us. As with healthy economic, social and other systems, your physical wellbeing can only be sustained through a life of communication with human and non-human others in a sentient landscape that will show you, if you pay attention, how to live in health and balance. Bush medicine works wonders, sure, but only in the bush. A plant can cure a condition when harvested in a particular place and season, especially when complemented with all the foods that are seasonal in its habitat, but it can't help you if it's plucked, crushed, packed and sent halfway round the world for you to gobble up anytime you like.

This is why being a shaman or medicine person is really difficult and unrewarding. People from all around the world come here seeking secret wisdom and magical powers from our Elders, and they inevitably return home either disappointed with, or lying about, what they've learned. These are hard facts which, on their own, can only sour into wrong story over time, so I will accompany them with a bit of a yarn about a magical bone.

Ten years ago in Western Australia an Elder gave me a whale vertebra. He said he'd found it half a century earlier, washed up on the shores of his country, and that his old people told him to keep it until the day he saw a boy with white owl story inside of him. He would be a lost and broken person, but he would know what to do with that bone. (I know—sounds like a fucking prophecy. I struggle with these red flags too.) The old man found me there decades later and said the blue whale backbone belonged to me. He told me the story and said I would know how to use it, and I have been carrying it around ever since.

I often wonder if he made a mistake. I never mentioned owl to him, so I thought it was a confirmation that he somehow knew I was the right boy, just by looking at me. That's not appropriate logic in Indigenous inquiry—something that may be coincidence or a mentalist trick can't be taken alone as a 'sign' to inform decision-making. There has to be a web of related connections that can be verified by different people of cultural authority, as well as a series of communications from non-human entities.

My scepticism in the decade since has resulted in excessive caution and the stalling of my cultural obligations as a keeper of this object. For a long time I found no connection in Lore between white owl and whale, so I doubted and procrastinated. I refused to examine some of my stories from southern Australia that I wished to remain forgotten, until I was forced this year to be guided into that country, on a journey that was unexpected. I was sung back in by custodians, through koala, waterfall, cave, stone, river, eagle and the big two-snakes story that connects across the continent, linking with first man first woman story, and their child. I cried a lot, and something shifted.

Tentative inquiry with the whale showed a connection between male and female white owl sacred sites I had been shown years ago in the east and west of Australia, massive stones made of white quartz. And here is the part of the story you cannot trust—the 'Jesus told me' moment. I can't verify this for you, but whale showed me a third site that has been submerged off the west coast since the time the oceans rose in the last dramatic period of climate change about twelve thousand years ago. The whale brought the knowledge of that owl place to the beach and died there so it could be picked up and passed on to reconnect the three sites. On that coast, beached whales often bring the spirits of unborn children from the drowned country under the sea to be carried inland and born through the fresh water.

I called the old fella and we spoke about the whale bone for the first time in years. I was excited about the whale talking to me, because I thought I had rekindled through ritual practice something long dead inside, but it was the old fella who had done the work, moved by land and sea. He revealed that he had kept a small piece of that bone. The week before, the day I had woken up to the submerged owl place, he had dropped that piece of bone into a deep trench off the west coast.

For years the whale breeding site there had not yielded high birth-rates, because the love song of the males had not been heard for a long time. There is a cave there in the sea that they once used to amplify the song at a perfect frequency for opening the reproductive organs of the females, compressed from a long season of deep dives beneath ice sheets. Within days, the song was sung again into that cave and it was so loud it could be heard by humans standing on the shore. This part of the story is verifiable, as he made sure the whole process was filmed, from the dropping of the bone to the singing of the song.

I took the whale bone with me this year to Turtle Island on the other side of the world. I did rituals with First People there, and at Niagara Falls we worked with tobacco in ceremony and feasted the bone together. In their way, you hold feasts for sacred objects to give them energy. It's a different way from my own, but right story requires accommodation of diverse narratives and viewpoints.

My Native Canadian sister, Melanie Goodchild, showed me a cave-bear tooth she had been given to carry, to maintain the story and knowledge of that extinct entity and retrieve that Lore forward to inform future systems design. She told me that when she accepted this heavy object, she developed an abscess and lost one of her own teeth. She said when you accept something from an animal to carry, it replaces a part of you. My beautiful Megan was there too, and she helped me to see that the vertebra decaying in my spine was part of the process of carrying that whale bone, that I needed to walk with the pain and let it inform the way I carried that sacred object.

This is right story. Parts of it are subjective and unverifiable, but even if it were factually false, it would still be right story. There are many verifiable facts in the world that are deployed in isolation as wrong story to damage creation, such as the absence of female chess grandmasters. The fact on its own might be true, but the narrative built on top of it is wrong story. In the same way, right story may contain images that are verified in records, or simply images that only exist in our minds. It is often difficult to know the difference between right story and wrong story, because intent and relationality are not easy to measure.

Meaning-making in this space can be vacuous and even dangerous if it leads you to diagnosis and treatment of problems with story that excludes other narratives, so I'm proceeding with respect and caution. If I dismiss the entire field of medicine in the pursuit of this work to heal myself, then I will have descended into pseudo-science, and that is not our tradition. We listen to everybody and take our time to act upon what is emergent.

Right there, that's the problem. Time is the problem. Who the hell has the time to live and make sense of the world in this way anymore? The alarm clock is ringing to wake me from the sleep I didn't get while writing, and I need to get my family ready for their day, make breakfast for them, clean the house, make appointments, recycle the rubbish, drive everyone where they need to go, take a handful of painkillers and then show up ready for work. It's that or live on the street, which is a lifestyle with even harsher schedules.

That's my despair talking, sibling. There's good crazy and bad crazy—this is bad crazy. I suffer and so I observe the world through a lens of suffering, perceiving only paths to annihilation. My friend Daniel Schmachtenberger tells me that if I were to fall in love again right now, I would look at the same datasets and perceive opportunities and bright futures. That would be good crazy (but only for a while— eventually it would become sociopathic optimism).

Sitting with this whale bone I've been wilfully ignoring now for years, I recall being in love, us-two being held in love together in the land. Ah, that honeymoon of connectedness that occurs in between periods of economic precarity and desperate marathons of labour! I recall it and feel it again, because it is not bound by a calendar and it is-was-will-be. The good crazy splashes across my grimy lens and I am able to perceive that my failure to work with owl and whale effectively is irrelevant, because they did their work anyway, through me. I've just been feeling disgruntled about my lack of individual agency in the process.

FIDELIO NO. 15 (DUET)

I cannot doubt it again
—my love—
this is true,
[illusion or]
not illusion
or a temporary elixir in the tides of my body.

My love is real
[in the tides]
and of course I do not feel it inside of me,
because it does not live there.

[inside of]
It does not live in you either,
my most intimate other,
my occupying nemesis,
my shimmering light.

[all around]
My love

and
[between us]
yours
is between us and all around.
[all around]

It is in our yesterday and tomorrow
[ever was]
as we struggle to seek it in the elusive today.
But there is no today,
[ever will be]
and our love is there in the moment,

when our hands met at the fire
and they meet there still.
We dreamed that dream there in that place,

[still]

and we were taller than trees
and made of southern lights
and they sang with us there,

[all our ancestors and descendants who know what it is
to love.]

This is real,
and it ever was and ever will be.

This altered state, this temporary insanity of love, allows me to see the parts of the story that I've ignored. I've been directed along a big songline, over and over, energising sites and connections and, more importantly, keeping others safe and supported while they do that work too. I have cut a dozen pieces off that whale bone over the years and made things out of those fragments for people who needed them. I've used a piece of it to burnish all my wooden tools and weapons over the years, working whale story into those objects. I haven't told that story, because it doesn't belong to me, but I still belong to it. My clan has a song for it, and I have danced it and breathed it and walked with it in embassy all over the world where those whales migrate. But I'm ungrateful. Maybe I think I deserve more than this, that I have individual rights and privileges that must be honoured, powers that must be feared? I don't. That's somebody else's Dreaming.

Us-two came through this journey by canoe across nine circles of developmental hell and, in this liminal moment of ego death right at the end, we might perceive a pattern in all the wrong lines and sick story, a little self-terminating algorithm at the heart of radicalisation.

The algorithm emerges from a sneaky line of code that whispers, 'I am greater than you, you are less than me.' It expands into the protocols of extremism, which lead an in-group to define itself through bad relation with an out-group—a group that is 'other' and must be punished. As this paranoid algorithm grazes selectively on datasets in the world, it inevitably achieves a singularity known as the fascist turn. At this stage of its life cycle, it drives the dominant in-group to perceive itself as an oppressed community, to become convinced that the marginalised others they seek to punish are actually a powerful group that is responsible for all suffering.

Religions carry the seeds of that algorithm and cultivate the singularity of fascism in their devotees. There are always evil outsiders who are opposite, and our opposition to them defines our religious identities and knowledge. All pseudo-science operates within this pattern, feeding the algorithm with more bad data, wrong story. Who are we? *We are not them.* What is truth? *Truth is the opposite of their knowledge.* What is our plan? *To disrupt their plans.* What do they plan to do? *Probably all the shitty things we're doing.* A rapture is always imminent—that glorious day when our deity or our movement will punish the outsiders and establish a thousand-year regime of sacred Law that will protect us and free us from accountability, while removing protection from our enemies and holding them eternally accountable. Our deity will send divine agents to deliver unto us this paradise of privilege, but guess what? The secret is *those angels are among us, and you are one of those chosen agents of God.* So arm yourselves. Stand down and stand by. Your family? Your community? *Unbelievers.* The enemy is in your home, on your screen and on your streets. The time of judgment has come.

You may sense this faith-perverting trap and seek refuge in spirituality, only to find yourself caught up in an occult religion where the hierarchies and agendas are hidden. Organised religions then become your out-group enemies, and their beliefs provide the oppositional frames for your *I am not them, therefore I am* philosophy, and you are bound once again. All roads lead to Rome.

In this sense, there is nothing spiritual or religious about Indigenous knowledge, which is just a peer-driven process of coming to understand all your relations (human and non-human) within creation. But how can we define this process without grounding the description in opposition to spirituality, science or religion? All stories are welcome around our fires, even those that define us as pagan, heathen, other. In the end, our knowledge is human knowledge, accountable to community, ancestors, descendants and the eternal Law of the land.

We need to recover this human knowledge for all people, because nature won't survive modernity until it ceases to be an abstract, separate entity and becomes land again, with all of us embedded within it. Mum's calling us home to have a nice lunch and do some chores, which we have to get done before sunset otherwise we'll be going to bed without dinner!

Brother Deen says I have to stop this canoe journey through hell now, that I'm prolonging my engagement with wrong story far longer than I needed to for this book, that I'm holding myself and you as the reader in an addictive feedback loop of despair and ghoulish voyeurism. Us-two are in bed with the devil here, and eventually we'll find ourselves doing something we're not entirely comfortable with. He says I need to cut this final chapter short—but not before I find a way to meet my cultural obligation to you and make sure you're safe and open to being in good relation with the world.

He travelled a long way to see me the other night, to clean me with leaves and smoke and tell me, 'This stops here.' I'm sending that smoke to you too, my sibling. This is not a 'throw away your sticks' moment—there are no miracle cures. It just breaks the wrong-story feedback loop long enough for you to step out of it. Don't linger here too long. Burn after reading. I am.

Brother Deen says I have to complete the process of burning the wrong-story objects I made for this book. I'm still hanging on to one of them and when he touched it, he felt it like a radioactive punch in the guts. It's a big war boomerang with all the wrong story and circles of hell described in this book carved into it with a stone knife. It's a beautiful piece, seductive and terrible. I've had to bind it with leaves until I type the last word of this book, and then I'll burn it and let it go. We can't defeat an empire if we have become dependent on it as source material for our critique, opposition and entertainment.

I'm sitting now with the boomerang Brother Deen made for me and it's not half as beautiful as the ones I make, but it is right story. It's like a portal to undiluted love and connection, and I can feel that as a substance flowing around and through me. My owl-like gaze flickers on briefly for the first time in years and I can see those flows. The whale bone is in front of me, and I've begun (at last) carving right story into it.

I'm compartmentalised, though. All this story sounds subjective and superstitious to the sceptical atheist in me, and to the struggling scholar trying to reconcile his inquiry with the self-in-relation that has been pushed into another box for code-switching purposes. I think it's because I've been code-switching in accordance with categories of science and knowledge that don't really exist except in a market-place of abstractions.

Indigenous knowledge doesn't fit into any of those categories, but touches all of them. I keep moving them around like playing cards to make sense of them and I always end up with three piles, from my limited perspective. Those piles are pseudo-science, authentic science and mad science.

Pseudo-science and mad science are predatory disciplines that exist in extractive relation to authentic scientific endeavour. On the pseudo side, bits of science are cherrypicked and deliberately misrepresented to suit various grifts, while on the mad side innovations are extracted from authentic science, then scaled and weaponised for power and profit. Authentic science is a genuinely collective commons of knowledge, although it is often defamed by the extractive disciplines as being corrupt and monolithic. I've done this myself, spending half my career depicting science as hostile to Indigenous methods of inquiry in an *I am not them, therefore I am* kind of way.

But what is science? It is a community with a long lineage, comprising members of almost every culture on the planet, collectively sharing inquiry in rigorous, rule-governed ways, with peers reviewing peers in distributed networks of autonomous institutions that aren't controlled by any single, centralised authority. That also sounds to me like a fairly good description of Indigenous knowledge processes. It has been a mistake for me to divide myself into different parts so I can interact with this infinitely diverse community that I thought was my enemy. Us-two have probably both done a lot of this in our lives and work, dis-integrating ourselves and our relationships for no good reason.

Us-two might feel like we've gone too far, inhaled too much wrong story and done too many wrong works to come back from the edge of damnation. But Brother Deen has an image on the boomerang he gave us. It shows a journey between two circles that doesn't end with A to B, but keeps looping back around again and again. The journey is one of inquiry, and this doesn't end with truth or failure then death—we continue in cycles of increase indefinitely, and broken circles become whole again in this way. It's not the case that we can't come back from this. It's the opposite—we can never cease coming back around to make things right, even if we want to stop.

I may be in crisis, but only in the sense that things are happening that I think should not be happening. I struggle against acceptance of my reality like an emu stuck in barbed wire who keeps trying to kick the guts out of the ranger with the wire-cutters. I might call out *oh my old people, how come thou fella hast been forsake me!* But most people do that, either right before they die or right before they acquire wisdom. Dying's easier, which is why so many of us choose it. But those of us who take that rapturous path should not be making decisions or telling stories that affect everyone else. And here's wisdom—every story affects everyone else. You're in relation to everyone and everything. Choosing death for yourself is choosing death for the world, and that's not a decision you can make on your own, just to avoid the heavy lifting of getting connected and getting wisdom.

Our ancestors, our gods, our prophets, our country, our spirit, our cosmos—however we want to see the community of entities beyond our waking sight—they don't care about our crying and suffering from the self-inflicted wounds of our narcissistic struggles against creation. They cannot comfort us, any more than they can stop sailing ships from landing on a beach. All they can do is nudge us-all towards the pattern of creation to find our symbiotic roles within it, in annoyingly vague and non-linear ways that can only be perceived through constant connection with the land and collective processing of that relation.

Us-two hold our breaths and exit the infernal story-scape we've been traversing, not quite sure what will happen. To our surprise, the air is breathable, and the stars are ones we recognise. We are still alive.

There comes a tapping. There is a wall of glass between us and that infernal world we have travelled together, and on the other side Sir Anthony Hopkins is recreating his classic scene from *Silence of the Lambs*. He is grinning through his Hannibal Lecter fangs at us. We approach, noticing a line painted on the ground that we know we can't cross. Sir Anthony is a stoic, and he grins in a way that is seductive but unsettling. His messianic gaze draws us right to the edge of the line.

'First principles, you-two. Read Marcus Aurelius. What is each thing within itself? What is its nature? What does it do, this civilisation you despise?'

'It kills people. It kills land,' you reply.

'No! That is incidental. What is the first and principal thing it does, what need does it serve by killing?'

'Matricidal rage. Fear of death. Tiny dicks…'

'No, it covets. That is its nature. And how do we begin to covet, you-two? Do we seek out things to covet? No. We begin by coveting what we see every day.'

You start swaying forward, mesmerised, and this worries me, because we know we're not supposed to touch the glass. I've got your hand, though, and I give it a squeeze and you squeeze back. Our eyes meet. There is resolve growing in the relational space between us, and we reach a silent agreement. Us-two turn away and go into the world.

He calls us little birds and tells us to fly away. He intends this as an insult that will wound us, make us want to return in our pride and ask him more questions through the glass.

But us-two are happy being little birds, so away we fly.

About the Cover Artist

Steve Yunkaporta is the author's *wuny* (older brother), a respected Wik artist and sculptor belonging to the Apalech Clan.

About the Author

Tyson Yunkaporta is an academic, an arts critic, and a researcher who is a member of the Apalech Clan in far north Queensland. He is the author of *Sand Talk: How Indigenous Thinking Can Save the World*, winner of the Small Publishers' Adult Book of the Year at the Australian Book Industry Awards and the Ansari Institute's Randa and Sherif Nasr Book Prize on Religion & the World, awarded to an author who explores global issues using Indigenous perspectives. He carves traditional tools and weapons and also works as a senior lecturer in Indigenous Knowledges at Deakin University in Melbourne. He lives in Melbourne, Australia.

Praise for *Right Story, Wrong Story*

'Yunkaporta's writing style is disarming in the best way possible, never speaking to the reader with anything except earnest camaraderie and effortlessly weaving between corny jokes, mythological allusion and rigorous cultural theory. . . . *Right Story, Wrong Story*, at its core, is an invitation to sit, listen and share space in your head with another human being for a while. It's compelling, it's refreshing and it's something I would recommend to anyone disillusioned with modernity and looking for a new perspective.' – *Readings Monthly* (Best Nonfiction of 2023)

Praise for Tyson Yunkaporta's *Sand Talk*

Winner, Small Publishers' Adult Book of the Year,
Australian Book Industry Awards, 2020

Winner, the Ansari Institute's Randa and Sherif Nasr Book Prize
on Religion & the World, United States, 2022

Shortlisted, Matt Richell Award for New Writer of the Year,
Australian Book Industry Awards, 2020

Shortlisted, Non-Fiction, Indie Book Awards, 2020

Longlisted, Booktopia Favourite Australian Book, 2020

Longlisted, Booksellers' Choice for Adult Nonfiction,
Australian Booksellers Association, 2020

Longlisted, Non-Fiction, Indie Book Awards,
Leading Edge, 2020

'Thought-provoking and unconventional.' – *New York Times*

'Startling . . . extraordinary . . . gives lessons in complexity.' – *The Alternative*

'Clever, funny, thought provoking, sensible and generous all at the same time. A must read!' – *Sydney Morning Herald*

'*Sand Talk* has helped convince me even more that the most powerful solution to our world's problems is to reconnect culture and nature. It's why we need to embrace First Nation's wisdom and accept stories, and their history, as part of our own and not maintain this false illusion of Anglo-centric and scientific superiority.' – *Wildlife in the Balance*

'An incredibly valuable book and I recommend setting aside dedicated time (preferably in nature) to "feel into" its wisdom— become part of the system rather than being an observer, as the author so rightly shares.' – *Think Like a Tree*

'Well-researched and deeply respectful of culture, but not afraid to suggest change and innovation, or highlight hypocrisy and racism even within Yunkaporta's personal experience of community. This struggle of "us versus them" thinking—or "greater than/less than", as he describes it—is at the heart of the book.' – *Off the Leash*

'An extraordinary invitation into the world of the Dreaming . . . Unheralded.' – Melissa Lucashenko, author of *Mullumbimby*, *Edenglassie*, and *Too Much Lip*

'Radical ideas, bursting with reason.' – Tara June Winch, author of *The Yield*